MW01289615

Westminster Shorter Catechism

With
Proof Texts
(ESV)

This Catechism was prepared by the Westminster Assembly in 1647, and adopted by the General Assembly of the Church of Scotland, 1648; by the Presbyterian Synod of New York and Philadelphia, May, 1788: and by nearly all the Calvinistic Presbyterian and Congregational Churches of the English tongue. It was translated into Greek, Hebrew, Arabic, and many other languages, and appeared in innumerable editions.

The English is conformed to the edition of the Presbyterian Board, compared with the London edition of 1658 and other older English and Scotch editions, which present no variations of any account.

Scripture quotations are from The Holy Bible, English Standard Version, copyright ©2001 by Crossway Bibles, a publishing ministry of Good News Publishers. Used by permission.

All rights reserved

Good News Publishers (including Crossway Bibles) is a not-for-profit organization that exists solely for the purpose of publishing the good news of the gospel and the truth of God's Word, the Bible.

This edition assembled and published

as an aid for study of the

Holy Bible.

The work is dedicated to God

and is offered in memory of

Rev. Robert H. Balsinger

by

Robert B. Balsinger

Lewis Center, OH 43035

2007

Text files for digitizing or reprinting are available upon request.

Q 76 Which is the ninth commandment? 160

Q 77 What is required in the ninth commandment? 161

Q 78 What is forbidden in the ninth commandment? 163

Q 79 Which is the tenth commandment? 164

Q 80 What is required in the tenth commandment? 165

Q 81 What is forbidden in the tenth commandment? 168

Q 82 Is any man able perfectly to keep the commandments of God? 169

Q 83 Are all transgressions of the law equally heinous? 170

Q 84 What doth every sin deserve? 172

Q 85 What doth God require of us, that we may escape his wrath and due to curse, us for sin? 173

Q 86 What is faith in Jesus Christ? 175

Q 87 What is repentance unto life? 177

Q 88 What are the outward and ordinary means whereby Christ communicateth to us the benefits of redemption? 180

Q 89 How is the Word made effectual to salvation? 181

Q 90 How is the Word to be read and heard, that it may become effectual to salvation? 183

Q 91. How do the sacraments become effectual means of salvation? 185

Q 92 What is a sacrament? 187

Q 93 Which are the sacraments of the New Testament? 189

Q 1 What is the chief end of man?

A Man's chief end is to glorify God[1], and to enjoy him forever.[2]

[1]A Prayer of David. Incline your ear, O LORD, and answer me, for I am poor and needy. Preserve my life, for I am godly; save your servant, who trusts in you--you are my God. Be gracious to me, O Lord, for to you do I cry all the day. Gladden the soul of your servant, for to you, O Lord, do I lift up my soul. For you, O Lord, are good and forgiving, abounding in steadfast love to all who call upon you. Give ear, O LORD, to my prayer; listen to my plea for grace. In the day of my trouble I call upon you, for you answer me. There is none like you among the gods, O Lord, nor are there any works like yours. All the nations you have made shall come and worship before you, O Lord, and shall glorify your name. For you are great and do wondrous things; you alone are God. Teach me your way, O LORD, that I may walk in your truth; unite my heart to fear your name. I give thanks to you, O Lord my God, with my whole heart, and I will glorify your name forever. For great is your steadfast love toward me; you have delivered my soul from the depths of Sheol. O God, insolent men have risen up against me; a band of ruthless men seeks my life, and they do not set you before them. But you, O Lord, are a God merciful and gracious, slow to anger and abounding in steadfast love and faithfulness. Turn to me and be gracious to me; give your strength to your servant, and save the son of your maidservant. Show me a sign of your favor, that those who hate me may see and be put to shame because you, LORD, have helped me and comforted me.

(Psalms 86:1-17)

Your people shall all be righteous; they shall possess the land forever, the branch of my planting, the work of my hands, that I might be glorified.

(Isaiah 60:21)

For from him and through him and to him are all things. To him be glory forever. Amen.

(Romans 11:36)

for you were bought with a price. So glorify God in your body.

(1 Corinthians 6:20)

So, whether you eat or drink, or whatever you do, do all to the glory of God.

(1 Corinthians 10:31)

(2) The LORD is my chosen portion and my cup; you hold my lot. The lines have fallen for me in pleasant places; indeed, I have a beautiful inheritance. I bless the LORD who gives me counsel; in the night also my heart instructs me. I have set the LORD always before me; because he is at my right hand, I shall not be shaken. Therefore my heart is glad, and my whole being rejoices; my flesh also dwells secure. For you will not abandon my soul to Sheol, or let your holy one see corruption. You make known to me the path of life; in your presence there is fullness of joy; at your right hand are pleasures forevermore.

(Psalms 16:5-11)

Blessed are the people to whom such blessings fall! Blessed are the people whose God is the LORD!

(Psalms 144:15)

"Behold, God is my salvation; I will trust, and will not be afraid; for the LORD GOD is my strength and my song, and he has become my salvation."

(Isaiah 12:2)

And the angel said to them, "Fear not, for behold, I bring you good news of great joy that will be for all the people.

(Luke 2:10)

Rejoice in the Lord always; again I will say, Rejoice.

(Philippians 4:4)

And I heard a loud voice from the throne saying, "Behold, the dwelling place of God is with man. He will dwell with them, and they will be his people, and God himself will be with them as their God. He will wipe away every tear from their eyes, and death shall be no more, neither shall there be mourning, nor crying, nor pain anymore, for the former things have passed away."

(Revelation 21:3-4)

Q 2 What rule hath God given to direct us how we may glorify and enjoy him?

A The Word of God, which is contained in the Scriptures of the Old and New Testaments (3) is the only rule to direct us how we may glorify and enjoy him (4)

(3)He answered, "Have you not read that he who created them from the beginning made them male and female, and said, 'Therefore a man shall leave his father and his mother and hold fast to his wife, and the two shall become one flesh'?

(Matthew 19:4-5)

Therefore a man shall leave his father and his mother and hold fast to his wife, and they shall become one flesh.

(Genesis 2:24)

And beginning with Moses and all the Prophets, he interpreted to them in all the Scriptures the things concerning himself.

(Luke 24:27)

Then he said to them, "These are my words that I spoke to you while I was still with you, that everything written about me in the Law of Moses and the Prophets and the Psalms must be fulfilled."

(Luke 24:44)

And we impart this in words not taught by human wisdom but taught by the Spirit, interpreting spiritual truths to those who are spiritual.

(1 Corinthians 2:13)

If anyone thinks that he is a prophet, or spiritual, he should acknowledge that the things I am writing to you are a command of the Lord.

(1 Corinthians 14:37)

knowing this first of all, that no prophecy of Scripture comes from someone's own interpretation. For no prophecy was ever produced by the will of man, but men spoke from God as they were carried along by the Holy Spirit.

(2 Peter 1:20-21)

that you should remember the predictions of the holy prophets and the commandment of the Lord and Savior through your apostles,

(2 Peter 3:2)

And count the patience of our Lord as salvation, just as our beloved brother Paul also wrote to you according to the wisdom given him, as he does in all his letters when he speaks in them of these matters. There are some things in them that are hard to understand, which the ignorant and unstable twist to their own destruction, as they do the other Scriptures.

(2 Peter 3:15-16)

(4) You shall not add to the word that I command you, nor take from it, that you may keep the commandments of the LORD your God that I command you.

(Deuteronomy 4:2)

The law of the LORD is perfect, reviving the soul; the testimony of the LORD is sure, making wise the simple; the precepts of the LORD are right, rejoicing the heart; the commandment of the LORD is pure, enlightening the eyes; the fear of the LORD is clean, enduring forever; the rules of the LORD are true, and righteous altogether. More to be desired are they than gold, even much fine gold; sweeter also than honey and drippings of the honeycomb. Moreover, by them is your servant warned; in keeping them there is great reward.

(Psalms 19:7-11)

To the teaching and to the testimony! If they will not speak according to this word, it is because they have no dawn.

(Isaiah 8:20)

These things I have spoken to you, that my joy may be in you, and that your joy may be full.

(John 15:11)

Now Jesus did many other signs in the presence of the disciples, which are not written in this book; but these are written so that you may believe that Jesus is the Christ, the Son of God, and that by believing you may have life in his name.

(John 20:30-31)

Now these Jews were more noble than those in Thessalonica; they received the word with all eagerness, examining the Scriptures daily to see if these things were so.

(Acts 17:11)

and how from childhood you have been acquainted with the sacred writings, which are able to make you wise for salvation through faith in Christ Jesus. All Scripture is breathed out by God and profitable for teaching, for reproof, for correction, and for training in righteousness, that the man of God may be competent, equipped for every good work.

(2 Timothy 3:15-17)

And we are writing these things so that our joy may be complete.

(1 John 1:4)

Q 3 What do the Scriptures principally teach?

A The Scriptures principally teach, what man is to believe concerning God,[5] and what duty God requires of man [6]

[5] In the beginning, God created the heavens and the earth.

(Genesis 1:1)

You search the Scriptures because you think that in them you have eternal life; and it is they that bear witness about me,

(John 5:39)

but these are written so that you may believe that Jesus is the Christ, the Son of God, and that by believing you may have life in his name.

(John 20:31)

So faith comes from hearing, and hearing through the word of Christ.

(Romans 10:17)

and how from childhood you have been acquainted with the sacred writings, which are able to make you wise for salvation through faith in Christ Jesus.

(2 Timothy 3:15)

[6]"And now, Israel, what does the LORD your God require of you, but to fear the LORD your God, to walk in all his ways, to love him, to serve the LORD

your God with all your heart and with all your soul, and to keep the commandments and statutes of the LORD, which I am commanding you today for your good?

(Deuteronomy 10:12-13)

This Book of the Law shall not depart from your mouth, but you shall meditate on it day and night, so that you may be careful to do according to all that is written in it. For then you will make your way prosperous, and then you will have good success.

(Joshua 1:8)

Your word is a lamp to my feet and a light to my path.

(Psalms 119:105)

He has told you, O man, what is good; and what does the LORD require of you but to do justice, and to love kindness, and to walk humbly with your God?

(Micah 6:8)

All Scripture is breathed out by God and profitable for teaching, for reproof, for correction, and for training in righteousness, that the man of God may be competent, equipped for every good work.

(2 Timothy 3:16-17)

Q 4 What is God?

A God is a Spirit,[7] **infinite,**[8] **eternal,**[9] **and unchangeable,**[10] **in his being,**[11] **wisdom,**[12] **power,**[13] **holiness,**[14] **justice,**[15] **goodness,**[16] **and truth.**[17]

[7]"Therefore watch yourselves very carefully. Since you saw no form on the day that the LORD spoke to you at Horeb out of the midst of the fire, beware lest you act corruptly by making a carved image for yourselves, in the form of any figure, the likeness of male or female, the likeness of any animal that is on the earth, the likeness of any winged bird that flies in the air, the likeness of anything that creeps on the ground, the likeness of any fish that is in the water under the earth. And beware lest you raise your eyes to heaven, and when you see the sun and the moon and the stars, all the host of heaven, you be drawn away and bow down to them and serve them, things that the LORD your God has allotted to all the peoples under the whole heaven.

(Deuteronomy 4:15-19)

See my hands and my feet, that it is I myself. Touch me, and see. For a spirit does not have flesh and bones as you see that I have."

(Luke 24:39)

No one has ever seen God; the only God, who is at the Father's side, he has made him known.

(John 1:18)

God is spirit, and those who worship him must worship in spirit and truth."

(John 4:24)

Being then God's offspring, we ought not to think that the divine being is like gold or silver or stone, an image formed by the art and imagination of man.

(Acts 17:29)

(8) "But will God indeed dwell on the earth? Behold, heaven and the highest heaven cannot contain you; how much less this house that I have built!

(1 Kings 8:27)

Where shall I go from your Spirit? Or where shall I flee from your presence?

(Psalms 139:7)

Great is the LORD, and greatly to be praised, and his greatness is unsearchable.

(Psalms 145:3)

Great is our Lord, and abundant in power; his understanding is beyond measure.

(Psalms 147:5)

Can a man hide himself in secret places so that I cannot see him? declares the LORD. Do I not fill heaven and earth? declares the LORD.

(Jeremiah 23:24)

Oh, the depth of the riches and wisdom and knowledge of God! How unsearchable are his judgments and how inscrutable his ways! "For who has known the mind of the Lord, or who has been his counselor?" "Or who has given a gift to him that he might be repaid?" For from him and through him and to him are all things. To him be glory forever. Amen.

(Romans 11:33-36)

The eternal God is your dwelling place, and underneath are the everlasting arms. And he thrust out the enemy before you and said, Destroy.

(Deuteronomy 33:27)

Before the mountains were brought forth, or ever you had formed the earth and the world, from everlasting to everlasting you are God.

(Psalms 90:2)

But you, O LORD, are enthroned forever; you are remembered throughout all generations.

(Psalms 102:12)

"O my God," I say, "take me not away in the midst of my days-- you whose years endure throughout all generations!" Of old you laid the foundation of the earth, and the heavens are the work of your hands. They will perish, but you will remain; they will all wear out like a garment. You will change them like a robe, and they will pass away, but you are the same, and your years have no end.

(Psalms 102:24-27)

John to the seven churches that are in Asia: Grace to you and peace from him who is and who was and who is to come, and from the seven spirits who are before his throne,

(Revelation 1:4)

(10)The counsel of the LORD stands forever, the plans of his heart to all generations.

(Psalms 33:11)

"For I the LORD do not change; therefore you, O children of Jacob, are not consumed.

(Malachi 3:6)

like a robe you will roll them up, like a garment they will be changed. But you are the same, and your years will have no end."

(Hebrews 1:12)

So when God desired to show more convincingly to the heirs of the promise the unchangeable character of his purpose, he guaranteed it with an oath, so that by two unchangeable things, in which it is impossible for God to lie, we who have fled for refuge might have strong encouragement to hold fast to the hope set before us.

(Hebrews 6:17-18)

Jesus Christ is the same yesterday and today and forever.

(Hebrews 13:8)

Every good gift and every perfect gift is from above, coming down from the Father of lights with whom there is no variation or shadow due to change.

(James 1:17)

(11) God said to Moses, "I AM WHO I AM." And he said, "Say this to the people of Israel, 'I AM has sent me to you.'"

(Exodus 3:14)

Why should the nations say, "Where is their God?"

(Psalms 115:2)

To the King of ages, immortal, invisible, the only God, be honor and glory forever and ever. Amen.

(1 Timothy 1:17)

which he will display at the proper time--he who is the blessed and only Sovereign, the King of kings and Lord of lords, who alone has immortality, who dwells in unapproachable light, whom no one has ever seen or can see. To him be honor and eternal dominion. Amen.

(1 Timothy 6:15-16)

(12) O LORD, how manifold are your works! In wisdom have you made them all; the earth is full of your creatures.

(Psalms 104:24)

Oh, the depth of the riches and wisdom and knowledge of God! How unsearchable are his judgments and how inscrutable his ways! "For who has known the mind of the Lord, or who has been his counselor?"

(Romans 11:33-34)

And no creature is hidden from his sight, but all are naked and exposed to the eyes of him to whom we must give account.

(Hebrews 4:13)

for whenever our heart condemns us, God is greater than our heart, and he knows everything.

(1 John 3:20)

(13)When Abram was ninety-nine years old the LORD appeared to Abram and said to him, "I am God Almighty; walk before me, and be blameless,

(Genesis 17:1)

Once God has spoken; twice have I heard this: that power belongs to God,

(Psalms 62:11)

'Ah, Lord GOD! It is you who have made the heavens and the earth by your great power and by your outstretched arm! Nothing is too hard for you.

(Jeremiah 32:17)

But Jesus looked at them and said, "With man this is impossible, but with God all things are possible."

(Matthew 19:26)

"I am the Alpha and the Omega," says the Lord God, "who is and who was and who is to come, the Almighty."

(Revelation 1:8)

(14) And to which of the angels has he ever said, "Sit at my right hand until I make your enemies a footstool for your feet"?

(Hebrews 1:13)

but as he who called you is holy, you also be holy in all your conduct, since it is written, "You shall be holy, for I am holy."

(1 Peter 1:15-16)

And everyone who thus hopes in him purifies himself as he is pure.

(1 John 3:3)

Who will not fear, O Lord, and glorify your name? For you alone are holy. All nations will come and worship you, for your righteous acts have been revealed."

(Revelation 15:4)

(15) Far be it from you to do such a thing, to put the righteous to death with the wicked, so that the righteous fare as the wicked! Far be that from you! Shall not the Judge of all the earth do what is just?"

(Genesis 18:25)

The LORD passed before him and proclaimed, "The LORD, the LORD, a God merciful and gracious, slow to anger, and abounding in steadfast love and faithfulness, keeping steadfast love for thousands, forgiving iniquity and transgression and sin, but who will by no means clear the guilty, visiting the iniquity of the fathers on the children and the children's children, to the third and the fourth generation."

(Exodus 34:6-7)

"The Rock, his work is perfect, for all his ways are justice. A God of faithfulness and without iniquity, just and upright is he.

(Deuteronomy 32:4)

before the LORD, for he comes, for he comes to judge the earth. He will judge the world in righteousness, and the peoples in his faithfulness.

(Psalms 96:13)

But if our unrighteousness serves to show the righteousness of God, what shall we say? That God is unrighteous to inflict wrath on us? (I speak in a human way.)

(Romans 3:5)

It was to show his righteousness at the present time, so that he might be just and the justifier of the one who has faith in Jesus.

(Romans 3:26)

(16) who satisfies you with good so that your youth is renewed like the eagle's.

(Psalms 103:5)

Let them thank the LORD for his steadfast love, for his wondrous works to the children of man!

(Psalms 107:8)

They said to him, "Why then did Moses command one to give a certificate of divorce and to send her away?"

(Matthew 19:7)

Or do you presume on the riches of his kindness and forbearance and patience, not knowing that God's kindness is meant to lead you to repentance?

(Romans 2:4)

(17) The LORD passed before him and proclaimed, "The LORD, the LORD, a God merciful and gracious, slow to anger, and abounding in steadfast love and faithfulness,

(Exodus 34:6)

"The Rock, his work is perfect, for all his ways are justice. A God of faithfulness and without iniquity, just and upright is he.

(Deuteronomy 32:4)

But you, O Lord, are a God merciful and gracious, slow to anger and abounding in steadfast love and faithfulness.

(Psalms 86:15)

For great is his steadfast love toward us, and the faithfulness of the LORD endures forever. Praise the LORD!

(Psalms 117:2)

so that by two unchangeable things, in which it is impossible for God to lie, we who have fled for refuge might have strong encouragement to hold fast to the hope set before us.

(Hebrews 6:18)

Q 5 Are there more Gods than one?

A There is but one only,[18] **the living and true God** [19]

[18] "Hear, O Israel: The LORD our God, the LORD is one.

(Deuteronomy 6:4)

Thus says the LORD, the King of Israel and his Redeemer, the LORD of hosts: "I am the first and I am the last; besides me there is no god.

(Isaiah 44:6)

Declare and present your case; let them take counsel together! Who told this long ago? Who declared it of old? Was it not I, the LORD? And there is no other god besides me, a righteous God and a Savior; there is none besides me. "Turn to me and be saved, all the ends of the earth! For I am God, and there is no other.

(Isaiah 45:21-22)

Therefore, as to the eating of food offered to idols, we know that "an idol has no real existence," and that "there is no God but one." For although there may be so-called gods in heaven or on earth--as indeed there are many "gods" and many "lords"-- yet for us there is one God, the Father, from whom are all things and for whom we exist, and one Lord, Jesus Christ, through whom are all things and through whom we exist.

(1 Corinthians 8:4-6)

[19] But the LORD is the true God; he is the living God and the everlasting King. At his wrath the earth quakes, and the nations cannot endure his indignation.

(Jeremiah 10:10)

And this is eternal life, that they know you the only true God, and Jesus Christ whom you have sent.

(John 17:3)

For they themselves report concerning us the kind of reception we had among you, and how you turned to God from idols to serve the living and true God,

(1 Thessalonians 1:9)

And we know that the Son of God has come and has given us understanding, so that we may know him who is true; and we are in him who is true, in his Son Jesus Christ. He is the true God and eternal life.

(1 John 5:20)

Q 6 How many persons are there in the Godhead?

A There are three persons in the Godhead: the Father, the Son, and the Holy Ghost;[20] and these three are one God, the same in substance, equal in power and glory [21]

[20]And when Jesus was baptized, immediately he went up from the water, and behold, the heavens were opened to him, and he saw the Spirit of God descending like a dove and coming to rest on him;

(Matthew 3:16)

Go therefore and make disciples of all nations, baptizing them in the name of the Father and of the Son and of the Holy Spirit,

(Matthew 28:19)

The grace of the Lord Jesus Christ and the love of God and the fellowship of the Holy Spirit be with you all.

(2 Corinthians 13:14)

according to the foreknowledge of God the Father, in the sanctification of the Spirit, for obedience to Jesus Christ and for sprinkling with his blood: May grace and peace be multiplied to you.

(1 Peter 1:2)

[21] Your throne, O God, is forever and ever. The scepter of your kingdom is a scepter of uprightness;

(Psalms 45:6)

In the beginning was the Word, and the Word was with God, and the Word was God.

(John 1:1)

And now, Father, glorify me in your own presence with the glory that I had with you before the world existed.

(John 17:5)

But Peter said, "Ananias, why has Satan filled your heart to lie to the Holy Spirit and to keep back for yourself part of the proceeds of the land? While it remained unsold, did it not remain your own? And after it was sold, was it not at your disposal? Why is it that you have contrived this deed in your heart? You have not lied to men but to God."

(Acts 5:3-4)

To them belong the patriarchs, and from their race, according to the flesh, is the Christ who is God over all, blessed forever. Amen.

(Romans 9:5)

For in him the whole fullness of deity dwells bodily,

(Colossians 2:9)

Now to him who is able to keep you from stumbling and to present you blameless before the presence of his glory with great joy,

(Jude 1:24)

Q 7 What are the decrees of God?

A The decrees of God are, his eternal purpose, according to the counsel of his will, whereby, for his own glory, he hath foreordained whatsoever comes to pass (22)

(22)The counsel of the LORD stands forever, the plans of his heart to all generations.

(Psalms 33:11)

The LORD of hosts has sworn: "As I have planned, so shall it be, and as I have purposed, so shall it stand,

(Isaiah 14:24)

this Jesus, delivered up according to the definite plan and foreknowledge of God, you crucified and killed by the hands of lawless men.

(Acts 2:23)

In him we have obtained an inheritance, having been predestined according to the purpose of him who works all things according to the counsel of his will, so that we who were the first to hope in Christ might be to the praise of his glory.

(Ephesians 1:11-12)

Q 8 How doth God execute his decrees?

A God executeth his decrees in the works of creation and providence [23]

[23]fire and hail, snow and mist, stormy wind fulfilling his word!

(Psalms 148:8)

Lift up your eyes on high and see: who created these? He who brings out their host by number, calling them all by name, by the greatness of his might, and because he is strong in power not one is missing.

(Isaiah 40:26)

all the inhabitants of the earth are accounted as nothing, and he does according to his will among the host of heaven and among the inhabitants of the earth; and none can stay his hand or say to him, "What have you done?"

(Daniel 4:35)

And when they heard it, they lifted their voices together to God and said, "Sovereign Lord, who made the heaven and the earth and the sea and everything in them, who through the mouth of our father David, your servant, said by the Holy Spirit, "'Why did the Gentiles rage, and the peoples plot in vain? The kings of the earth set themselves, and the rulers were gathered together, against the Lord and against his Anointed'-- for truly in this city there were gathered together against your holy servant Jesus, whom you anointed, both Herod and Pontius Pilate, along with the Gentiles and the peoples of Israel, to do whatever your hand and your plan had predestined to take place.

(Acts 4:24-28)

"Worthy are you, our Lord and God, to receive glory and honor and power, for you created all things, and by your will they existed and were created."

(Revelation 4:11)

Q 9 What is the work of creation?

A The work of creation is, God's making all things of nothing, by the word of his power,(24) in the space of six days, and all very good (25)

(24)In the beginning, God created the heavens and the earth.

(Genesis 1:1)

By the word of the LORD the heavens were made, and by the breath of his mouth all their host.

(Psalms 33:6)

For he spoke, and it came to be; he commanded, and it stood firm.

(Psalms 33:9)

By faith we understand that the universe was created by the word of God, so that what is seen was not made out of things that are visible.

(Hebrews 11:3)

(25) And God saw everything that he had made, and behold, it was very good. And there was evening and there was morning, the sixth day.

(Genesis 1:31)

Q 10 How did God create man?

A God created man male and female, after his own image,[26] **in knowledge,**[27] **righteousness, and holiness,**[28] **with dominion over the creatures** [29]

[26] So God created man in his own image, in the image of God he created him; male and female he created them.

(Genesis 1:27)

[27] and have put on the new self, which is being renewed in knowledge after the image of its creator.

(Colossians 3:10)

[28] and to put on the new self, created after the likeness of God in true righteousness and holiness.

(Ephesians 4:24)

[29] And God blessed them. And God said to them, "Be fruitful and multiply and fill the earth and subdue it and have dominion over the fish of the sea and over the birds of the heavens and over every living thing that moves on the earth."

(Genesis 1:28)

To the choirmaster: according to The Gittith. A Psalm of David. O LORD, our Lord, how majestic is your name in all the earth! You have set your glory above the heavens. Out of the mouth of babies and infants, you have established strength because of your foes, to still the enemy and the avenger. When I look at your heavens, the work of your fingers, the moon and the stars, which you have set in place, what is man that you are mindful of him, and the son of man that you care for him? Yet you have made him a little lower than the heavenly beings and crowned him with glory and honor. You have given him dominion over the works of your hands; you have put all things under his feet, all sheep and oxen, and also the beasts of the field, the birds of the heavens, and the fish of the sea, whatever passes along the paths of the seas. O LORD, our Lord, how majestic is your name in all the earth!

(Psalms 8:1-9)

Q 11 What are God's works of providence?

A God's works of providence are, his most holy,[30] wise,[31] and powerful[32] preserving[33] and governing[34] all his creatures, and all their actions [35]

[30] The LORD is righteous in all his ways and kind in all his works.

(Psalms 145:17)

[31]O LORD, how manifold are your works! In wisdom have you made them all; the earth is full of your creatures.

(Psalms 104:24)

[32] He is the radiance of the glory of God and the exact imprint of his nature, and he upholds the universe by the word of his power. After making purification for sins, he sat down at the right hand of the Majesty on high,

(Hebrews 1:3)

[33] "You are the LORD, you alone. You have made heaven, the heaven of heavens, with all their host, the earth and all that is on it, the seas and all that is in them; and you preserve all of them; and the host of heaven worships you.

(Nehemiah 9:6)

[34] and what is the immeasurable greatness of his power toward us who believe, according to the working of his great might that he worked in Christ when he raised him from the dead and seated him at his right hand in the heavenly places, far above all rule and authority and power and dominion, and above every name that is named, not only in this age but also in the one to come. And

he put all things under his feet and gave him as head over all things to the church,

(Ephesians 1:19-22)

(35) Your righteousness is like the mountains of God; your judgments are like the great deep; man and beast you save, O LORD.

(Psalms 36:6)

The lot is cast into the lap, but its every decision is from the LORD.

(Proverbs 16:33)

But even the hairs of your head are all numbered.

(Matthew 10:30)

Q 12 What special act of providence did God exercise towards man in the estate wherein he was created?

A **When God had created man, he entered into a covenant of life with him, upon condition of perfect obedience; forbidding him to eat of the tree of the knowledge of good and evil, upon pain of death** (36)

(36)And the LORD God commanded the man, saying, "You may surely eat of every tree of the garden, but of the tree of the knowledge of good and evil you shall not eat, for in the day that you eat of it you shall surely die."

(Genesis 2:16-17)

For whoever keeps the whole law but fails in one point has become accountable for all of it.

(James 2:10)

Q 13 Did our first parents continue in the estate wherein they were created?

A Our first parents, being left to the freedom of their own will, fell from the estate wherein they were created, by sinning against God (37)

(37) So when the woman saw that the tree was good for food, and that it was a delight to the eyes, and that the tree was to be desired to make one wise, she took of its fruit and ate, and she also gave some to her husband who was with her, and he ate. Then the eyes of both were opened, and they knew that they were naked. And they sewed fig leaves together and made themselves loincloths. And they heard the sound of the LORD God walking in the garden in the cool of the day, and the man and his wife hid themselves from the presence of the LORD God among the trees of the garden.

(Genesis 3:6-8)

Then the LORD God said to the woman, "What is this that you have done?" The woman said, "The serpent deceived me, and I ate."

(Genesis 3:13)

But I am afraid that as the serpent deceived Eve by his cunning, your thoughts will be led astray from a sincere and pure devotion to Christ.

(2 Corinthians 11:3)

Q 14 What is sin?

A Sin is any want of conformity unto, or transgression of, the law of God (38)

(38)"If anyone sins, doing any of the things that by the LORD's commandments ought not to be done, though he did not know it, then realizes his guilt, he shall bear his iniquity.

(Leviticus 5:17)

So whoever knows the right thing to do and fails to do it, for him it is sin.

(James 4:17)

Everyone who makes a practice of sinning also practices lawlessness; sin is lawlessness.

(1 John 3:4)

Q 15 What was the sin whereby our first parents fell from the estate wherein they were created?

A The sin whereby our first parents fell from the estate wherein they were created, was their eating the forbidden fruit [39]

So when the woman saw that the tree was good for food, and that it was a delight to the eyes, and that the tree was to be desired to make one wise, she took of its fruit and ate, and she also gave some to her husband who was with her, and he ate.

(Genesis 3:6)

Q 16 Did all mankind fall in Adam's first transgression?

A The covenant being made with Adam,(40) not only for himself, but for his posterity; all mankind, descending from him by ordinary generation, sinned in him, and fell with him, in his first transgression (41)

(40)And the LORD God commanded the man, saying, "You may surely eat of every tree of the garden, but of the tree of the knowledge of good and evil you shall not eat, for in the day that you eat of it you shall surely die."

(Genesis 2:16-17)

For whoever keeps the whole law but fails in one point has become accountable for all of it.

(James 2:10)

(41) Therefore, just as sin came into the world through one man, and death through sin, and so death spread to all men because all sinned-- for sin indeed was in the world before the law was given, but sin is not counted where there is no law. Yet death reigned from Adam to Moses, even over those whose sinning was not like the transgression of Adam, who was a type of the one who was to come. But the free gift is not like the trespass. For if many died through one man's trespass, much more have the grace of God and the free gift by the grace of that one man Jesus Christ abounded for many. And the free gift is not like the result of that one man's sin. For the judgment following one trespass brought condemnation, but the free gift following many trespasses brought justification. For if, because of one man's trespass, death reigned through that one man, much more will those who receive the abundance of grace and the free gift of righteousness reign in life through the one man Jesus Christ. Therefore, as one trespass led to condemnation for all men, so one act of righteousness leads to justification and life for all men. For as by the one man's disobedience the many were made sinners, so by the one man's obedience the many will be made righteous. Now the law came in to increase the trespass, but where sin increased, grace abounded all the more, so that, as sin reigned in

death, grace also might reign through righteousness leading to eternal life through Jesus Christ our Lord.

(Romans 5:12-21)

For as in Adam all die, so also in Christ shall all be made alive.

(1 Corinthians 15:22)

Q 17 Into what estate did the fall bring mankind?

A The fall brought mankind into an estate of sin and misery (42)

(42) To the woman he said, "I will surely multiply your pain in childbearing; in pain you shall bring forth children. Your desire shall be for your husband, and he shall rule over you." And to Adam he said, "Because you have listened to the voice of your wife and have eaten of the tree of which I commanded you, 'You shall not eat of it,' cursed is the ground because of you; in pain you shall eat of it all the days of your life; thorns and thistles it shall bring forth for you; and you shall eat the plants of the field. By the sweat of your face you shall eat bread, till you return to the ground, for out of it you were taken; for you are dust, and to dust you shall return."

(Genesis 3:16-19)

To the woman he said, "I will surely multiply your pain in childbearing; in pain you shall bring forth children. Your desire shall be for your husband, and he shall rule over you."

(Genesis 3:16)

in their paths are ruin and misery,

(Romans 3:16)

Therefore, just as sin came into the world through one man, and death through sin, and so death spread to all men because all sinned--

(Romans 5:12)

And you were dead in the trespasses and sins

(Ephesians 2:1)

Q 18 Wherein consists the sinfulness of that estate whereinto man fell?

A The sinfulness of that estate whereinto man fell, consists in the guilt of Adam's first sin,[43] the want of original righteousness,[44] and the corruption of his whole nature,[45] which is commonly called original sin; together with all actual transgressions which proceed from it [46]

[43]Therefore, just as sin came into the world through one man, and death through sin, and so death spread to all men because all sinned--

(Romans 5:12)

For as by the one man's disobedience the many were made sinners, so by the one man's obedience the many will be made righteous.

(Romans 5:19)

[44] as it is written: "None is righteous, no, not one;

(Romans 3:10)

and have put on the new self, which is being renewed in knowledge after the image of its creator.

(Colossians 3:10)

and to put on the new self, created after the likeness of God in true righteousness and holiness.

(Ephesians 4:24)

(45) Behold, I was brought forth in iniquity, and in sin did my mother conceive me.

(Psalms 51:5)

That which is born of the flesh is flesh, and that which is born of the Spirit is spirit.

(John 3:6)

"There is no fear of God before their eyes."

(Romans 3:18)

For the mind that is set on the flesh is hostile to God, for it does not submit to God's law; indeed, it cannot. Those who are in the flesh cannot please God.

(Romans 8:7-8)

among whom we all once lived in the passions of our flesh, carrying out the desires of the body and the mind, and were by nature children of wrath, like the rest of mankind.

(Ephesians 2:3)

(46) The LORD saw that the wickedness of man was great in the earth, and that every intention of the thoughts of his heart was only evil continually.

(Genesis 6:5)

To the choirmaster: according to Mahalath. A Maskil of David. The fool says in his heart, "There is no God." They are corrupt, doing abominable iniquity; there is none who does good.

(Psalms 53:1)

For out of the heart come evil thoughts, murder, adultery, sexual immorality, theft, false witness, slander.

(Matthew 15:19)

as it is written: "None is righteous, no, not one; no one understands; no one seeks for God. All have turned aside; together they have become worthless; no one does good, not even one." "Their throat is an open grave; they use their tongues to deceive." "The venom of asps is under their lips." "Their mouth is full of curses and bitterness." "Their feet are swift to shed blood; in their paths are ruin and misery, and the way of peace they have not known." "There is no fear of God before their eyes."

(Romans 3:10-18)

for all have sinned and fall short of the glory of God,

(Romans 3:23)

Now the works of the flesh are evident: sexual immorality, impurity, sensuality, idolatry, sorcery, enmity, strife, jealousy, fits of anger, rivalries, dissensions, divisions, envy, drunkenness, orgies, and things like these. I warn you, as I warned you before, that those who do such things will not inherit the kingdom of God.

(Galatians 5:19-21)

But each person is tempted when he is lured and enticed by his own desire. Then desire when it has conceived gives birth to sin, and sin when it is fully grown brings forth death.

(James 1:14-15)

Q 19 What is the misery of that estate whereinto man fell?

A All mankind by their fall lost communion with God,(47) are under his wrath(48) and curse,(49) and so made liable to all the miseries of this life,(50) to death(51) itself, and to the pains of hell forever (52)

(47)And they heard the sound of the LORD God walking in the garden in the cool of the day, and the man and his wife hid themselves from the presence of the LORD God among the trees of the garden.

(Genesis 3:8)

He drove out the man, and at the east of the garden of Eden he placed the cherubim and a flaming sword that turned every way to guard the way to the tree of life.

(Genesis 3:24)

Jesus answered them, "Truly, truly, I say to you, everyone who commits sin is a slave to sin.

(John 8:34)

Jesus said to them, "If God were your Father, you would love me, for I came from God and I am here. I came not of my own accord, but he sent me.

(John 8:42)

You are of your father the devil, and your will is to do your father's desires. He was a murderer from the beginning, and has nothing to do with the truth, because there is no truth in him. When he lies, he speaks out of his own character, for he is a liar and the father of lies.

(John 8:44)

remember that you were at that time separated from Christ, alienated from the commonwealth of Israel and strangers to the covenants of promise, having no hope and without God in the world.

(Ephesians 2:12)

They are darkened in their understanding, alienated from the life of God because of the ignorance that is in them, due to their hardness of heart.

(Ephesians 4:18)

(48) Whoever believes in the Son has eternal life; whoever does not obey the Son shall not see life, but the wrath of God remains on him.

(John 3:36)

For the wrath of God is revealed from heaven against all ungodliness and unrighteousness of men, who by their unrighteousness suppress the truth.

(Romans 1:18)

among whom we all once lived in the passions of our flesh, carrying out the desires of the body and the mind, and were by nature children of wrath, like the rest of mankind.

(Ephesians 2:3)

Let no one deceive you with empty words, for because of these things the wrath of God comes upon the sons of disobedience.

(Ephesians 5:6)

(49) For all who rely on works of the law are under a curse; for it is written, "Cursed be everyone who does not abide by all things written in the Book of the Law, and do them."

(Galatians 3:10)

No longer will there be anything accursed, but the throne of God and of the Lamb will be in it, and his servants will worship him.

(Revelation 22:3)

(50) To the woman he said, "I will surely multiply your pain in childbearing; in pain you shall bring forth children. Your desire shall be for your husband, and he shall rule over you." And to Adam he said, "Because you have listened to the voice of your wife and have eaten of the tree of which I commanded you, 'You shall not eat of it,' cursed is the ground because of you; in pain you shall eat of it all the days of your life; thorns and thistles it shall bring forth for you; and you shall eat the plants of the field. By the sweat of your face you shall eat bread, till you return to the ground, for out of it you were taken; for you are dust, and to dust you shall return."

(Genesis 3:16-19)

but man is born to trouble as the sparks fly upward.

(Job 5:7)

What has a man from all the toil and striving of heart with which he toils beneath the sun? For all his days are full of sorrow, and his work is a vexation. Even in the night his heart does not rest. This also is vanity.

(Ecclesiastes 2:22-23)

For I consider that the sufferings of this present time are not worth comparing with the glory that is to be revealed to us. For the creation waits with eager longing for the revealing of the sons of God. For the creation was subjected to futility, not willingly, but because of him who subjected it, in hope that the creation itself will be set free from its bondage to corruption and obtain the freedom of the glory of the children of God. For we know that the whole creation has been groaning together in the pains of childbirth until now. And not only the creation, but we ourselves, who have the firstfruits of the Spirit, groan inwardly as we wait eagerly for adoption as sons, the redemption of our bodies.

(Romans 8:18-23)

(51) Behold, all souls are mine; the soul of the father as well as the soul of the son is mine: the soul who sins shall die.

(Ezekiel 18:4)

Therefore, just as sin came into the world through one man, and death through sin, and so death spread to all men because all sinned--

(Romans 5:12)

For the wages of sin is death, but the free gift of God is eternal life in Christ Jesus our Lord.

(Romans 6:23)

"Then he will say to those on his left, 'Depart from me, you cursed, into the eternal fire prepared for the devil and his angels.

(Matthew 25:41)

And these will go away into eternal punishment, but the righteous into eternal life."

(Matthew 25:46)

(52) They will suffer the punishment of eternal destruction, away from the presence of the Lord and from the glory of his might,

(2 Thessalonians 1:9)

And another angel, a third, followed them, saying with a loud voice, "If anyone worships the beast and its image and receives a mark on his forehead or on his hand, he also will drink the wine of God's wrath, poured full strength into the cup of his anger, and he will be tormented with fire and sulfur in the presence of the holy angels and in the presence of the Lamb. And the smoke of their torment goes up forever and ever, and they have no rest, day or night, these worshipers of the beast and its image, and whoever receives the mark of its name."

(Revelation 14:9-11)

Q 20 Did God leave all mankind to perish in the estate of sin and misery?

A God, having out of his mere good pleasure, from all eternity, elected some to everlasting life,(53) did enter into a covenant of grace to deliver them out of the estate of sin and misery, and to bring them into an estate of salvation by a Redeemer (54)

(53) And when the Gentiles heard this, they began rejoicing and glorifying the word of the Lord, and as many as were appointed to eternal life believed.

(Acts 13:48)

even as he chose us in him before the foundation of the world, that we should be holy and blameless before him. In love he predestined us for adoption as sons through Jesus Christ, according to the purpose of his will,

(Ephesians 1:4-5)

But we ought always to give thanks to God for you, brothers beloved by the Lord, because God chose you as the firstfruits to be saved, through sanctification by the Spirit and belief in the truth. To this he called you through our gospel, so that you may obtain the glory of our Lord Jesus Christ.

(2 Thessalonians 2:13-14)

(54) I will put enmity between you and the woman, and between your offspring and her offspring; he shall bruise your head, and you shall bruise his heel."

(Genesis 3:15)

And I will establish my covenant between me and you and your offspring after you throughout their generations for an everlasting covenant, to be God to you and to your offspring after you.

(Genesis 17:7)

Now therefore, if you will indeed obey my voice and keep my covenant, you shall be my treasured possession among all peoples, for all the earth is mine; and you shall be to me a kingdom of priests and a holy nation. These are the words that you shall speak to the people of Israel."

(Exodus 19:5-6)

But everyone shall die for his own sin. Each man who eats sour grapes, his teeth shall be set on edge. "Behold, the days are coming, declares the LORD, when I will make a new covenant with the house of Israel and the house of Judah, not like the covenant that I made with their fathers on the day when I took them by the hand to bring them out of the land of Egypt, my covenant that they broke, though I was their husband, declares the LORD. But this is the covenant that I will make with the house of Israel after those days, declares the LORD: I will put my law within them, and I will write it on their hearts. And I will be their God, and they shall be my people. And no longer shall each one teach his neighbor and each his brother, saying, 'Know the LORD,' for they shall all know me, from the least of them to the greatest, declares the LORD. For I will forgive their iniquity, and I will remember their sin no more."

(Jeremiah 31:30-34)

even as the Son of Man came not to be served but to serve, and to give his life as a ransom for many."

(Matthew 20:28)

In the same way also he took the cup, after supper, saying, "This cup is the new covenant in my blood. Do this, as often as you drink it, in remembrance of me."

(1 Corinthians 11:25)

Therefore he is the mediator of a new covenant, so that those who are called may receive the promised eternal inheritance, since a death has occurred that redeems them from the transgressions committed under the first covenant.

(Hebrews 9:15)

Q 21 Who is the Redeemer of God's elect?

A The only Redeemer of God's elect is the Lord Jesus Christ,[55] **who, being the eternal Son of God,**[56] **became man,**[57] **and so was, and continueth to be, God and man in two distinct natures, and one person, forever** [58]

[55] Jesus said to him, "I am the way, and the truth, and the life. No one comes to the Father except through me.

(John 14:6)

And there is salvation in no one else, for there is no other name under heaven given among men by which we must be saved."

(Acts 4:12)

For there is one God, and there is one mediator between God and men, the man Christ Jesus, who gave himself as a ransom for all, which is the testimony given at the proper time.

(1 Timothy 2:5-6)

[56] I will tell of the decree: The LORD said to me, "You are my Son; today I have begotten you.

(Psalms 2:7)

and behold, a voice from heaven said, "This is my beloved Son, with whom I am well pleased."

(Matthew 3:17)

He was still speaking when, behold, a bright cloud overshadowed them, and a voice from the cloud said, "This is my beloved Son, with whom I am well pleased; listen to him."

(Matthew 17:5)

No one has ever seen God; the only God, who is at the Father's side, he has made him known.

(John 1:18)

(57) For to us a child is born, to us a son is given; and the government shall be upon his shoulder, and his name shall be called Wonderful Counselor, Mighty God, Everlasting Father, Prince of Peace.

(Isaiah 9:6)

"Behold, the virgin shall conceive and bear a son, and they shall call his name Immanuel" (which means, God with us).

(Matthew 1:23)

And the Word became flesh and dwelt among us, and we have seen his glory, glory as of the only Son from the Father, full of grace and truth.

(John 1:14)

But when the fullness of time had come, God sent forth his Son, born of woman, born under the law,

(Galatians 4:4)

(58) and said, "Men of Galilee, why do you stand looking into heaven? This Jesus, who was taken up from you into heaven, will come in the same way as you saw him go into heaven."

(Acts 1:11)

but he holds his priesthood permanently, because he continues forever. Consequently, he is able to save to the uttermost those who draw near to God through him, since he always lives to make intercession for them.

(Hebrews 7:24-25)

Q 22 How did Christ, being the Son of God, become man?

A Christ, the Son of God, became man, by taking to himself a true body, and a reasonable soul,(59) being conceived by the power of the Holy Ghost, in the womb of the virgin Mary, and born of her,(60) yet without sin (61)

(59) but made himself nothing, taking the form of a servant, being born in the likeness of men.

(Philippians 2:7)

Since therefore the children share in flesh and blood, he himself likewise partook of the same things, that through death he might destroy the one who has the power of death, that is, the devil,

(Hebrews 2:14)

Therefore he had to be made like his brothers in every respect, so that he might become a merciful and faithful high priest in the service of God, to make propitiation for the sins of the people.

(Hebrews 2:17)

(60) to a virgin betrothed to a man whose name was Joseph, of the house of David. And the virgin's name was Mary.

(Luke 1:27)

And behold, you will conceive in your womb and bear a son, and you shall call his name Jesus.

(Luke 1:31)

And the angel answered her, "The Holy Spirit will come upon you, and the power of the Most High will overshadow you; therefore the child to be born will be called holy--the Son of God.

(Luke 1:35)

[61]For our sake he made him to be sin who knew no sin, so that in him we might become the righteousness of God.

(2 Corinthians 5:21)

For we do not have a high priest who is unable to sympathize with our weaknesses, but one who in every respect has been tempted as we are, yet without sin.

(Hebrews 4:15)

For it was indeed fitting that we should have such a high priest, holy, innocent, unstained, separated from sinners, and exalted above the heavens.

(Hebrews 7:26)

You know that he appeared to take away sins, and in him there is no sin.

(1 John 3:5)

Q 23 What offices doth Christ execute as our Redeemer?

A Christ, as our Redeemer, executeth the offices of a prophet,(62) of a priest,(63) and of a king,(64) both in his estate of humiliation and exaltation

(62) I will raise up for them a prophet like you from among their brothers. And I will put my words in his mouth, and he shall speak to them all that I command him.

(Deuteronomy 18:18)

Being therefore exalted at the right hand of God, and having received from the Father the promise of the Holy Spirit, he has poured out this that you yourselves are seeing and hearing.

(Acts 2:33)

Moses said, 'The Lord God will raise up for you a prophet like me from your brothers. You shall listen to him in whatever he tells you. And it shall be that every soul who does not listen to that prophet shall be destroyed from the people.'

(Acts 3:22-23)

Long ago, at many times and in many ways, God spoke to our fathers by the prophets, but in these last days he has spoken to us by his Son, whom he appointed the heir of all things, through whom also he created the world.

(Hebrews 1:1-2)

(63) Since then we have a great high priest who has passed through the heavens, Jesus, the Son of God, let us hold fast our confession. For we do not have a high priest who is unable to sympathize with our weaknesses, but one who in every respect has been tempted as we are, yet without sin.

(Hebrews 4:14-15)

So also Christ did not exalt himself to be made a high priest, but was appointed by him who said to him, "You are my Son, today I have begotten you"; as he says also in another place, "You are a priest forever, after the order of Melchizedek."

(Hebrews 5:5-6)

(64) For to us a child is born, to us a son is given; and the government shall be upon his shoulder, and his name shall be called Wonderful Counselor, Mighty God, Everlasting Father, Prince of Peace. Of the increase of his government and of peace there will be no end, on the throne of David and over his kingdom, to establish it and to uphold it with justice and with righteousness from this time forth and forevermore. The zeal of the LORD of hosts will do this.

(Isaiah 9:6-7)

He will be great and will be called the Son of the Most High. And the Lord God will give to him the throne of his father David, and he will reign over the house of Jacob forever, and of his kingdom there will be no end."

(Luke 1:32-33)

Then Pilate said to him, "So you are a king?" Jesus answered, "You say that I am a king. For this purpose I was born and for this purpose I have come into the world--to bear witness to the truth. Everyone who is of the truth listens to my voice."

(John 18:37)

For he must reign until he has put all his enemies under his feet.

(1 Corinthians 15:25)

Q 24 How doth Christ execute the office of a prophet?

A Christ executeth the office of a prophet, in revealing to us, by his Word[65] and Spirit,[66] the will of God for our salvation [67]

[65]"The Spirit of the Lord is upon me, because he has anointed me to proclaim good news to the poor. He has sent me to proclaim liberty to the captives and recovering of sight to the blind, to set at liberty those who are oppressed, to proclaim the year of the Lord's favor."

(Luke 4:18-19)

And he began to say to them, "Today this Scripture has been fulfilled in your hearing."

(Luke 4:21)

In the first book, O Theophilus, I have dealt with all that Jesus began to do and teach, until the day when he was taken up, after he had given commands through the Holy Spirit to the apostles whom he had chosen.

(Acts 1:1-2)

how shall we escape if we neglect such a great salvation? It was declared at first by the Lord, and it was attested to us by those who heard,

(Hebrews 2:3)

[66] "But when the Helper comes, whom I will send to you from the Father, the Spirit of truth, who proceeds from the Father, he will bear witness about me.

And you also will bear witness, because you have been with me from the beginning.

(John 15:26-27)

But you will receive power when the Holy Spirit has come upon you, and you will be my witnesses in Jerusalem and in all Judea and Samaria, and to the end of the earth."

(Acts 1:8)

inquiring what person or time the Spirit of Christ in them was indicating when he predicted the sufferings of Christ and the subsequent glories.

(1 Peter 1:11)

[67] And many more believed because of his word. They said to the woman, "It is no longer because of what you said that we believe, for we have heard for ourselves, and we know that this is indeed the Savior of the world."

(John 4:41-42)

Now Jesus did many other signs in the presence of the disciples, which are not written in this book; but these are written so that you may believe that Jesus is the Christ, the Son of God, and that by believing you may have life in his name.

(John 20:30-31)

Q 25 How doth Christ execute the office of a priest?

A Christ executeth the office of a priest, in his once offering up of himself a sacrifice to satisfy divine justice,[68] and reconcile us to God,[69] and in making continual intercession for us [70]

[68]Who has believed what he has heard from us? And to whom has the arm of the LORD been revealed? For he grew up before him like a young plant, and like a root out of dry ground; he had no form or majesty that we should look at him, and no beauty that we should desire him. He was despised and rejected by men; a man of sorrows, and acquainted with grief; and as one from whom men hide their faces he was despised, and we esteemed him not. Surely he has borne our griefs and carried our sorrows; yet we esteemed him stricken, smitten by God, and afflicted. But he was wounded for our transgressions; he was crushed for our iniquities; upon him was the chastisement that brought us peace, and with his stripes we are healed. All we like sheep have gone astray; we have turned--every one--to his own way; and the LORD has laid on him the iniquity of us all. He was oppressed, and he was afflicted, yet he opened not his mouth; like a lamb that is led to the slaughter, and like a sheep that before its shearers is silent, so he opened not his mouth. By oppression and judgment he was taken away; and as for his generation, who considered that he was cut off out of the land of the living, stricken for the transgression of my people? And they made his grave with the wicked and with a rich man in his death, although he had done no violence, and there was no deceit in his mouth. Yet it was the will of the LORD to crush him; he has put him to grief; when his soul makes an offering for guilt, he shall see his offspring; he shall prolong his days; the will of the LORD shall prosper in his hand. Out of the anguish of his soul he shall see and be satisfied; by his knowledge shall the righteous one, my servant, make many to be accounted righteous, and he shall bear their iniquities. Therefore I will divide him a portion with the many, and he shall divide the spoil with the strong, because he poured out his soul to death and was numbered with the transgressors; yet he bore the sin of many, and makes intercession for the transgressors.

(Isaiah 53:1-12)

Now the passage of the Scripture that he was reading was this: "Like a sheep he was led to the slaughter and like a lamb before its shearer is silent, so he opens not his mouth. In his humiliation justice was denied him. Who can describe his generation? For his life is taken away from the earth." And the eunuch said to Philip, "About whom, I ask you, does the prophet say this, about himself or about someone else?" Then Philip opened his mouth, and beginning with this Scripture he told him the good news about Jesus.

(Acts 8:32-35)

for then he would have had to suffer repeatedly since the foundation of the world. But as it is, he has appeared once for all at the end of the ages to put away sin by the sacrifice of himself. And just as it is appointed for man to die once, and after that comes judgment, so Christ, having been offered once to bear the sins of many, will appear a second time, not to deal with sin but to save those who are eagerly waiting for him.

(Hebrews 9:26-28)

But when Christ had offered for all time a single sacrifice for sins, he sat down at the right hand of God,

(Hebrews 10:12)

[69] For if while we were enemies we were reconciled to God by the death of his Son, much more, now that we are reconciled, shall we be saved by his life. More than that, we also rejoice in God through our Lord Jesus Christ, through whom we have now received reconciliation.

(Romans 5:10-11)

All this is from God, who through Christ reconciled us to himself and gave us the ministry of reconciliation;

(2 Corinthians 5:18)

And you, who once were alienated and hostile in mind, doing evil deeds, he has now reconciled in his body of flesh by his death, in order to present you holy and blameless and above reproach before him,

(Colossians 1:21-22)

(70)Who is to condemn? Christ Jesus is the one who died--more than that, who was raised--who is at the right hand of God, who indeed is interceding for us.

(Romans 8:34)

Consequently, he is able to save to the uttermost those who draw near to God through him, since he always lives to make intercession for them.

(Hebrews 7:25)

For Christ has entered, not into holy places made with hands, which are copies of the true things, but into heaven itself, now to appear in the presence of God on our behalf.

(Hebrews 9:24)

Q 26 How doth Christ execute the office of a king?

A Christ executeth the office of a king, in subduing us to himself, in ruling and defending us,[71] and in restraining and conquering all his and our enemies [72]

[71] Your people will offer themselves freely on the day of your power, in holy garments; from the womb of the morning, the dew of your youth will be yours.

(Psalms 110:3)

And Jesus came and said to them, "All authority in heaven and on earth has been given to me. Go therefore and make disciples of all nations, baptizing them in the name of the Father and of the Son and of the Holy Spirit, teaching them to observe all that I have commanded you. And behold, I am with you always, to the end of the age."

(Matthew 28:18-20)

since you have given him authority over all flesh, to give eternal life to all whom you have given him.

(John 17:2)

He has delivered us from the domain of darkness and transferred us to the kingdom of his beloved Son,

(Colossians 1:13)

[72] "As for me, I have set my King on Zion, my holy hill." I will tell of the decree: The LORD said to me, "You are my Son; today I have begotten you.

Ask of me, and I will make the nations your heritage, and the ends of the earth your possession. You shall break them with a rod of iron and dash them in pieces like a potter's vessel."

(Psalms 2:6-9)

A Psalm of David. The LORD says to my Lord: "Sit at my right hand, until I make your enemies your footstool." The LORD sends forth from Zion your mighty scepter. Rule in the midst of your enemies!

(Psalms 110:1-2)

But if it is by the Spirit of God that I cast out demons, then the kingdom of God has come upon you.

(Matthew 12:28)

Then comes the end, when he delivers the kingdom to God the Father after destroying every rule and every authority and power. For he must reign until he has put all his enemies under his feet. The last enemy to be destroyed is death.

(1 Corinthians 15:24-26)

He disarmed the rulers and authorities and put them to open shame, by triumphing over them in him.

(Colossians 2:15)

Q 27 Wherein did Christ's humiliation consist?

A Christ's humiliation consisted in his being born, and that in a low condition,[73] **made under the law,**[74] **undergoing the miseries of this life,**[75] **the wrath of God,**[76] **and the cursed death of the cross;**[77] **in being buried, and continuing under the power of death for a time** [78]

[73]And she gave birth to her firstborn son and wrapped him in swaddling cloths and laid him in a manger, because there was no place for them in the inn.

(Luke 2:7)

For you know the grace of our Lord Jesus Christ, that though he was rich, yet for your sake he became poor, so that you by his poverty might become rich.

(2 Corinthians 8:9)

But when the fullness of time had come, God sent forth his Son, born of woman, born under the law,

(Galatians 4:4)

[74] But when the fullness of time had come, God sent forth his Son, born of woman, born under the law,

(Galatians 4:4)

[75] He was despised and rejected by men; a man of sorrows, and acquainted with grief; and as one from whom men hide their faces he was despised, and we esteemed him not.

(Isaiah 53:3)

And Jesus said to him, "Foxes have holes, and birds of the air have nests, but the Son of Man has nowhere to lay his head."

(Luke 9:58)

Jacob's well was there; so Jesus, wearied as he was from his journey, was sitting beside the well. It was about the sixth hour.

(John 4:6)

Jesus wept.

(John 11:35)

For because he himself has suffered when tempted, he is able to help those who are being tempted.

(Hebrews 2:18)

(76) To the choirmaster: according to The Doe of the Dawn. A Psalm of David. My God, my God, why have you forsaken me? Why are you so far from saving me, from the words of my groaning?

(Psalms 22:1)

And about the ninth hour Jesus cried out with a loud voice, saying, "Eli, Eli, lema sabachthani?" that is, "My God, my God, why have you forsaken me?"

(Matthew 27:46)

Yet it was the will of the LORD to crush him; he has put him to grief; when his soul makes an offering for guilt, he shall see his offspring; he shall prolong his days; the will of the LORD shall prosper in his hand.

(Isaiah 53:10)

He is the propitiation for our sins, and not for ours only but also for the sins of the whole world.

(1 John 2:2)

(77) Christ redeemed us from the curse of the law by becoming a curse for us-- for it is written, "Cursed is everyone who is hanged on a tree"--

(Galatians 3:13)

And being found in human form, he humbled himself by becoming obedient to the point of death, even death on a cross.

(Philippians 2:8)

(78) For just as Jonah was three days and three nights in the belly of the great fish, so will the Son of Man be three days and three nights in the heart of the earth.

(Matthew 12:40)

For I delivered to you as of first importance what I also received: that Christ died for our sins in accordance with the Scriptures, that he was buried, that he was raised on the third day in accordance with the Scriptures,

(1 Corinthians 15:3-4)

Q 28 Wherein consisteth Christ's exaltation?

A Christ's exaltation consisteth in his rising again from the dead on the third day,(79) in ascending up into heaven,(80) in sitting at the right hand(81) of God the Father, and in coming to judge the world at the last day (82)

(79) that he was buried, that he was raised on the third day in accordance with the Scriptures,

(1 Corinthians 15:4)

(80) You ascended on high, leading a host of captives in your train and receiving gifts among men, even among the rebellious, that the LORD God may dwell there.

(Psalms 68:18)

and said, "Men of Galilee, why do you stand looking into heaven? This Jesus, who was taken up from you into heaven, will come in the same way as you saw him go into heaven."

(Acts 1:11)

Therefore it says, "When he ascended on high he led a host of captives, and he gave gifts to men."

(Ephesians 4:8)

(81) A Psalm of David. The LORD says to my Lord: "Sit at my right hand, until I make your enemies your footstool."

(Psalms 110:1)

Being therefore exalted at the right hand of God, and having received from the Father the promise of the Holy Spirit, he has poured out this that you yourselves are seeing and hearing. For David did not ascend into the heavens, but he himself says, "'The Lord said to my Lord, Sit at my right hand,

(Acts 2:33-34)

He is the radiance of the glory of God and the exact imprint of his nature, and he upholds the universe by the word of his power. After making purification for sins, he sat down at the right hand of the Majesty on high,

(Hebrews 1:3)

(82) For the Son of Man is going to come with his angels in the glory of his Father, and then he will repay each person according to what he has done.

(Matthew 16:27)

because he has fixed a day on which he will judge the world in righteousness by a man whom he has appointed; and of this he has given assurance to all by raising him from the dead."

(Acts 17:31)

Q 29 How are we made partakers of the redemption purchased by Christ?

A We are made partakers of the redemption purchased by Christ, by the effectual application of it to us by his Holy Spirit [83]

[83]But when the goodness and loving kindness of God our Savior appeared, he saved us, not because of works done by us in righteousness, but according to his own mercy, by the washing of regeneration and renewal of the Holy Spirit, whom he poured out on us richly through Jesus Christ our Savior, so that being justified by his grace we might become heirs according to the hope of eternal life.

(Titus 3:4-7)

Q 30 How doth the Spirit apply to us the redemption purchased by Christ?

A The Spirit applieth to us the redemption purchased by Christ, by working faith in us,(84) and thereby uniting us to Christ in our effectual calling (85)

(84) So faith comes from hearing, and hearing through the word of Christ.

(Romans 10:17)

Now we have received not the spirit of the world, but the Spirit who is from God, that we might understand the things freely given us by God.

(1 Corinthians 2:12)

For by grace you have been saved through faith. And this is not your own doing; it is the gift of God,

(Ephesians 2:8)

For it has been granted to you that for the sake of Christ you should not only believe in him but also suffer for his sake,

(Philippians 1:29)

(85) I am the vine; you are the branches. Whoever abides in me and I in him, he it is that bears much fruit, for apart from me you can do nothing.

(John 15:5)

God is faithful, by whom you were called into the fellowship of his Son, Jesus Christ our Lord.

(1 Corinthians 1:9)

so that Christ may dwell in your hearts through faith--that you, being rooted and grounded in love,

(Ephesians 3:17)

Q 31 What is effectual calling?

A Effectual calling is the work of God's Spirit, whereby, convincing us of our sin and misery, enlightening our minds in the knowledge of Christ,(86) and renewing our wills,(87) he doth persuade and enable us to embrace Jesus Christ,(88) freely offered to us in the gospel (89)

(86) to open their eyes, so that they may turn from darkness to light and from the power of Satan to God, that they may receive forgiveness of sins and a place among those who are sanctified by faith in me.'

(Acts 26:18)

these things God has revealed to us through the Spirit. For the Spirit searches everything, even the depths of God.

(1 Corinthians 2:10)

Now we have received not the spirit of the world, but the Spirit who is from God, that we might understand the things freely given us by God.

(1 Corinthians 2:12)

For God, who said, "Let light shine out of darkness," has shone in our hearts to give the light of the knowledge of the glory of God in the face of Jesus Christ.

(2 Corinthians 4:6)

that the God of our Lord Jesus Christ, the Father of glory, may give you a spirit of wisdom and of revelation in the knowledge of him, having the eyes of your hearts enlightened, that you may know what is the hope to which he has called you, what are the riches of his glorious inheritance in the saints,

(Ephesians 1:17-18)

(87) And the LORD your God will circumcise your heart and the heart of your offspring, so that you will love the LORD your God with all your heart and with all your soul, that you may live.

(Deuteronomy 30:6)

And I will give you a new heart, and a new spirit I will put within you. And I will remove the heart of stone from your flesh and give you a heart of flesh. And I will put my Spirit within you, and cause you to walk in my statutes and be careful to obey my rules.

(Ezekiel 36:26-27)

Jesus answered, "Truly, truly, I say to you, unless one is born of water and the Spirit, he cannot enter the kingdom of God.

(John 3:5)

he saved us, not because of works done by us in righteousness, but according to his own mercy, by the washing of regeneration and renewal of the Holy Spirit,

(Titus 3:5)

(88) No one can come to me unless the Father who sent me draws him. And I will raise him up on the last day. It is written in the Prophets, 'And they will all be taught by God.' Everyone who has heard and learned from the Father comes to me--

(John 6:44-45)

One who heard us was a woman named Lydia, from the city of Thyatira, a seller of purple goods, who was a worshiper of God. The Lord opened her heart to pay attention to what was said by Paul.

(Acts 16:14)

[89]"Turn to me and be saved, all the ends of the earth! For I am God, and there is no other.

(Isaiah 45:22)

Come to me, all who labor and are heavy laden, and I will give you rest. Take my yoke upon you, and learn from me, for I am gentle and lowly in heart, and you will find rest for your souls. For my yoke is easy, and my burden is light."

(Matthew 11:28-30)

The Spirit and the Bride say, "Come." And let the one who hears say, "Come." And let the one who is thirsty come; let the one who desires take the water of life without price.

(Revelation 22:17)

Q 32 What benefits do they that are effectually called partake of in this life?

A They that are effectually called do in this life partake of justification, adoption, and sanctification, and the several benefits which in this life do either accompany or flow from them (90)

(90) And those whom he predestined he also called, and those whom he called he also justified, and those whom he justified he also glorified.

(Romans 8:30)

And because of him you are in Christ Jesus, who became to us wisdom from God, righteousness and sanctification and redemption,

(1 Corinthians 1:30)

And such were some of you. But you were washed, you were sanctified, you were justified in the name of the Lord Jesus Christ and by the Spirit of our God.

(1 Corinthians 6:11)

he predestined us for adoption as sons through Jesus Christ, according to the purpose of his will,

(Ephesians 1:5)

Q 33 What is justification?

A Justification is an act of God's free grace,[91] **wherein he pardoneth all our sins,**[92] **and accepteth us as righteous in His sight,**[93] **only for the righteousness of Christ imputed to us,**[94] **and received by faith alone** [95]

[91] and are justified by his grace as a gift, through the redemption that is in Christ Jesus,

(Romans 3:24)

[92] just as David also speaks of the blessing of the one to whom God counts righteousness apart from works: "Blessed are those whose lawless deeds are forgiven, and whose sins are covered; blessed is the man against whom the Lord will not count his sin."

(Romans 4:6-8)

that is, in Christ God was reconciling the world to himself, not counting their trespasses against them, and entrusting to us the message of reconciliation.

(2 Corinthians 5:19)

[93] For our sake he made him to be sin who knew no sin, so that in him we might become the righteousness of God.

(2 Corinthians 5:21)

[94] just as David also speaks of the blessing of the one to whom God counts righteousness apart from works:

(Romans 4:6)

He received the sign of circumcision as a seal of the righteousness that he had by faith while he was still uncircumcised. The purpose was to make him the father of all who believe without being circumcised, so that righteousness would be counted to them as well,

(Romans 4:11)

For as by the one man's disobedience the many were made sinners, so by the one man's obedience the many will be made righteous.

(Romans 5:19)

[95] yet we know that a person is not justified by works of the law but through faith in Jesus Christ, so we also have believed in Christ Jesus, in order to be justified by faith in Christ and not by works of the law, because by works of the law no one will be justified.

(Galatians 2:16)

and be found in him, not having a righteousness of my own that comes from the law, but that which comes through faith in Christ, the righteousness from God that depends on faith--

(Philippians 3:9)

Q 34 What is adoption?

A Adoption is an act of God's free grace,a whereby we are received into the number, and have a right to all the privileges, of the sons of God [96]

[96] See what kind of love the Father has given to us, that we should be called children of God; and so we are. The reason why the world does not know us is that it did not know him.

(1 John 3:1)

Q 35 What is sanctification?

A Sanctification is the work of God's free grace,[97] **whereby we are renewed in the whole man after the image of God,**[98] **and are enabled more and more to die unto sin, and live unto righteousness** [99]

[97] And I will put my Spirit within you, and cause you to walk in my statutes and be careful to obey my rules.

(Ezekiel 36:27)

for it is God who works in you, both to will and to work for his good pleasure.

(Philippians 2:13)

But we ought always to give thanks to God for you, brothers beloved by the Lord, because God chose you as the firstfruits to be saved, through sanctification by the Spirit and belief in the truth.

(2 Thessalonians 2:13)

[98] Therefore, if anyone is in Christ, he is a new creation. The old has passed away; behold, the new has come.

(2 Corinthians 5:17)

and to be renewed in the spirit of your minds, and to put on the new self, created after the likeness of God in true righteousness and holiness.

(Ephesians 4:23-24)

Now may the God of peace himself sanctify you completely, and may your whole spirit and soul and body be kept blameless at the coming of our Lord Jesus Christ.

(1 Thessalonians 5:23)

(99) I will sprinkle clean water on you, and you shall be clean from all your uncleannesses, and from all your idols I will cleanse you. And I will give you a new heart, and a new spirit I will put within you. And I will remove the heart of stone from your flesh and give you a heart of flesh. And I will put my Spirit within you, and cause you to walk in my statutes and be careful to obey my rules.

(Ezekiel 36:25-27)

We were buried therefore with him by baptism into death, in order that, just as Christ was raised from the dead by the glory of the Father, we too might walk in newness of life.

(Romans 6:4)

We know that our old self was crucified with him in order that the body of sin might be brought to nothing, so that we would no longer be enslaved to sin.

(Romans 6:6)

Let not sin therefore reign in your mortal body, to make you obey its passions. Do not present your members to sin as instruments for unrighteousness, but present yourselves to God as those who have been brought from death to life, and your members to God as instruments for righteousness. For sin will have no dominion over you, since you are not under law but under grace.

(Romans 6:12-14)

Since we have these promises, beloved, let us cleanse ourselves from every defilement of body and spirit, bringing holiness to completion in the fear of God.

(2 Corinthians 7:1)

He himself bore our sins in his body on the tree, that we might die to sin and live to righteousness. By his wounds you have been healed.

(1 Peter 2:24)

Q 36 What are the benefits which in this life do accompany or flow from justification, adoption, and sanctification?

A The benefits which in this life do accompany or flow from justification, adoption, and sanctification, are, assurance of God's love,(100) peace of conscience,(101) joy in the Holy Ghost,(102) increase of grace,(103) and perseverance therein to the end (104)

(100)and hope does not put us to shame, because God's love has been poured into our hearts through the Holy Spirit who has been given to us.

(Romans 5:5)

(101) Therefore, since we have been justified by faith, we have peace with God through our Lord Jesus Christ.

(Romans 5:1)

(102) For the kingdom of God is not a matter of eating and drinking but of righteousness and peace and joy in the Holy Spirit.

(Romans 14:17)

(103) But grow in the grace and knowledge of our Lord and Savior Jesus Christ. To him be the glory both now and to the day of eternity. Amen.

(2 Peter 3:18)

[104] And I am sure of this, that he who began a good work in you will bring it to completion at the day of Jesus Christ.

(Philippians 1:6)

who by God's power are being guarded through faith for a salvation ready to be revealed in the last time.

(1 Peter 1:5)

Q 37 What benefits do believers receive from Christ at death?

A The souls of believers are at their death made perfect in holiness,[105] **and do immediately pass into glory;**[106] **and their bodies, being still united in Christ,**[107] **do rest in their graves, till the resurrection** [108]

[105] and to the assembly of the firstborn who are enrolled in heaven, and to God, the judge of all, and to the spirits of the righteous made perfect,

(Hebrews 12:23)

[106] And he said to him, "Truly, I say to you, today you will be with me in Paradise."

(Luke 23:43)

So we are always of good courage. We know that while we are at home in the body we are away from the Lord,

(2 Corinthians 5:6)

Yes, we are of good courage, and we would rather be away from the body and at home with the Lord.

(2 Corinthians 5:8)

I am hard pressed between the two. My desire is to depart and be with Christ, for that is far better.

(Philippians 1:23)

(107) For since we believe that Jesus died and rose again, even so, through Jesus, God will bring with him those who have fallen asleep.

(1 Thessalonians 4:14)

(108) And many of those who sleep in the dust of the earth shall awake, some to everlasting life, and some to shame and everlasting contempt.

(Daniel 12:2)

Do not marvel at this, for an hour is coming when all who are in the tombs will hear his voice and come out, those who have done good to the resurrection of life, and those who have done evil to the resurrection of judgment.

(John 5:28-29)

having a hope in God, which these men themselves accept, that there will be a resurrection of both the just and the unjust.

(Acts 24:15)

Q 38 What benefits do believers receive from Christ at the resurrection?

A At the resurrection, believers, being raised up in glory,[109] **shall be openly acknowledged and acquitted in the day of judgment,**[110] **and made perfectly blessed in the full enjoying of God**[111] **to all eternity** [112]

[109] So is it with the resurrection of the dead. What is sown is perishable; what is raised is imperishable. It is sown in dishonor; it is raised in glory. It is sown in weakness; it is raised in power.

(1 Corinthians 15:42-43)

[110] And he will place the sheep on his right, but the goats on the left. Then the King will say to those on his right, 'Come, you who are blessed by my Father, inherit the kingdom prepared for you from the foundation of the world.

(Matthew 25:33-34)

And these will go away into eternal punishment, but the righteous into eternal life."

(Matthew 25:46)

[111] For those whom he foreknew he also predestined to be conformed to the image of his Son, in order that he might be the firstborn among many brothers.

(Romans 8:29)

Beloved, we are God's children now, and what we will be has not yet appeared; but we know that when he appears we shall be like him, because we shall see him as he is.

(1 John 3:2)

(112)You make known to me the path of life; in your presence there is fullness of joy; at your right hand are pleasures forevermore.

(Psalms 16:11)

Then we who are alive, who are left, will be caught up together with them in the clouds to meet the Lord in the air, and so we will always be with the Lord.

(1 Thessalonians 4:17)

Q 39 What is the duty which God requireth of man?

A The duty which God requireth of man, is obedience to his revealed will (113)

(113) "The secret things belong to the LORD our God, but the things that are revealed belong to us and to our children forever, that we may do all the words of this law.

(Deuteronomy 29:29)

He has told you, O man, what is good; and what does the LORD require of you but to do justice, and to love kindness, and to walk humbly with your God?

(Micah 6:8)

By this we know that we love the children of God, when we love God and obey his commandments. For this is the love of God, that we keep his commandments. And his commandments are not burdensome.

(1 John 5:2-3)

Q 40 What did God at first reveal to man for the rule of his obedience?

A The rule which God at first revealed to man for his obedience, was the moral law [114]

[114] For when Gentiles, who do not have the law, by nature do what the law requires, they are a law to themselves, even though they do not have the law. They show that the work of the law is written on their hearts, while their conscience also bears witness, and their conflicting thoughts accuse or even excuse them

(Romans 2:14-15)

For Moses writes about the righteousness that is based on the law, that the person who does the commandments shall live by them.

(Romans 10:5)

Q 41 Wherein is the moral law summarily comprehended?

A The moral law is summarily comprehended in the ten commandments
(115)

(115) And he declared to you his covenant, which he commanded you to perform, that is, the Ten Commandments, and he wrote them on two tablets of stone.

(Deuteronomy 4:13)

And he said to him, "Why do you ask me about what is good? There is only one who is good. If you would enter life, keep the commandments." He said to him, "Which ones?" And Jesus said, "You shall not murder, You shall not commit adultery, You shall not steal, You shall not bear false witness, Honor your father and mother, and, You shall love your neighbor as yourself."

(Matthew 19:17-19)

Q 42 What is the sum of the ten commandments?

A The sum of the ten commandments is, to love the Lord our God with all our heart, with all our soul, with all our strength, and with all our mind; and our neighbor as ourselves (116)

(116) And he said to him, "You shall love the Lord your God with all your heart and with all your soul and with all your mind. This is the great and first commandment. And a second is like it: You shall love your neighbor as yourself. On these two commandments depend all the Law and the Prophets."

(Matthew 22:37-40)

Q 43 What is the preface to the ten commandments?

A The preface to the ten commandments is in these words, I am the Lord thy God, which have brought thee out of the land of Egypt, out of the house of bondage (117)

(117) "I am the LORD your God, who brought you out of the land of Egypt, out of the house of slavery.

(Exodus 20:2)

"'I am the LORD your God, who brought you out of the land of Egypt, out of the house of slavery.

(Deuteronomy 5:6)

Q 44 What doth the preface to the ten commandments teach us?

A The preface to the ten commandments teacheth us, that because God is the Lord, and our God, and Redeemer, therefore we are bound to keep all his commandments (118)

(118) that we, being delivered from the hand of our enemies, might serve him without fear, in holiness and righteousness before him all our days.

(Luke 1:74-75)

As obedient children, do not be conformed to the passions of your former ignorance, but as he who called you is holy, you also be holy in all your conduct, since it is written, "You shall be holy, for I am holy." And if you call on him as Father who judges impartially according to each one's deeds, conduct yourselves with fear throughout the time of your exile, knowing that you were ransomed from the futile ways inherited from your forefathers, not with perishable things such as silver or gold, but with the precious blood of Christ, like that of a lamb without blemish or spot.

(1 Peter 1:14-19)

Q 45 Which is the first commandment?

A The first commandment is, Thou shalt have no other gods before me
(119)

(119)"You shall have no other gods before me.

(Exodus 20:3)

"'You shall have no other gods before me.

(Deuteronomy 5:7)

Q 46 What is required in the first commandment?

A The first commandment requireth us to know and acknowledge God to be the only true God, and our God; and to worship and glorify him accordingly (120)

(120) "And you, Solomon my son, know the God of your father and serve him with a whole heart and with a willing mind, for the LORD searches all hearts and understands every plan and thought. If you seek him, he will be found by you, but if you forsake him, he will cast you off forever.

(1 Chronicles 28:9)

"Assemble yourselves and come; draw near together, you survivors of the nations! They have no knowledge who carry about their wooden idols, and keep on praying to a god that cannot save. Declare and present your case; let them take counsel together! Who told this long ago? Who declared it of old? Was it not I, the LORD? And there is no other god besides me, a righteous God and a Savior; there is none besides me. "Turn to me and be saved, all the ends of the earth! For I am God, and there is no other. By myself I have sworn; from my mouth has gone out in righteousness a word that shall not return: 'To me every knee shall bow, every tongue shall swear allegiance.' "Only in the LORD, it shall be said of me, are righteousness and strength; to him shall come and be ashamed all who were incensed against him. In the LORD all the offspring of Israel shall be justified and shall glory."

(Isaiah 45:20-25)

Then Jesus said to him, "Be gone, Satan! For it is written, "'You shall worship the Lord your God and him only shall you serve.'"

(Matthew 4:10)

Q 47 What is forbidden in the first commandment?

A The first commandment forbiddeth the denying,(121) or not worshiping and glorifying, the true God as God,(122) and our God;(123) and the giving of that worship and glory to any other, which is due to him alone (124)

(121) To the choirmaster. Of David. The fool says in his heart, "There is no God." They are corrupt, they do abominable deeds, there is none who does good.

(Psalms 14:1)

(122) For his invisible attributes, namely, his eternal power and divine nature, have been clearly perceived, ever since the creation of the world, in the things that have been made. So they are without excuse.

(Romans 1:20)

(123) I am the LORD your God, who brought you up out of the land of Egypt. Open your mouth wide, and I will fill it. "But my people did not listen to my voice; Israel would not submit to me.

(Psalms 81:10-11)

(124) And he brought me into the inner court of the house of the LORD. And behold, at the entrance of the temple of the LORD, between the porch and the altar, were about twenty-five men, with their backs to the temple of the LORD, and their faces toward the east, worshiping the sun toward the east. Then he said to me, "Have you seen this, O son of man? Is it too light a thing for the house of Judah to commit the abominations that they commit here, that they should fill the land with violence and provoke me still further to anger? Behold, they put the branch to their nose. Therefore I will act in wrath. My eye will not spare, nor will I have pity. And though they cry in my ears with a loud voice, I will not hear them."

(Ezekiel 8:16-18)

because they exchanged the truth about God for a lie and worshiped and served the creature rather than the Creator, who is blessed forever! Amen.

(Romans 1:25)

Q 48 What are we specially taught by these words before me in the first commandment?

A These words before me in the first commandment teach us, that God, who seeth all things, taketh notice of, and is much displeased with, the sin of having any other God (125)

(125) But if your heart turns away, and you will not hear, but are drawn away to worship other gods and serve them, I declare to you today, that you shall surely perish. You shall not live long in the land that you are going over the Jordan to enter and possess.

(Deuteronomy 30:17-18)

If we had forgotten the name of our God or spread out our hands to a foreign god, would not God discover this? For he knows the secrets of the heart.

(Psalms 44:20-21)

Then he said to me, "Son of man, have you seen what the elders of the house of Israel are doing in the dark, each in his room of pictures? For they say, 'The LORD does not see us, the LORD has forsaken the land.'"

(Ezekiel 8:12)

Q 49 Which is the second commandment?

A Thou shalt not make unto thee any graven image, or any likeness of any thing that is in heaven above, or that is in the earth beneath, or that is in the water under the earth: Thou shalt not bow down thyself to them, nor serve them: for I the LORD thy God am a jealous God, visiting the iniquity of the fathers upon the children unto the third and fourth generation of them that hate me; And shewing mercy unto thousands of them that love me, and keep my commandments (126)

(126) "You shall not make for yourself a carved image, or any likeness of anything that is in heaven above, or that is in the earth beneath, or that is in the water under the earth. You shall not bow down to them or serve them, for I the LORD your God am a jealous God, visiting the iniquity of the fathers on the children to the third and the fourth generation of those who hate me, but showing steadfast love to thousands of those who love me and keep my commandments.

(Exodus 20:4-6)

"'You shall not make for yourself a carved image, or any likeness of anything that is in heaven above, or that is on the earth beneath, or that is in the water under the earth. You shall not bow down to them or serve them; for I the LORD your God am a jealous God, visiting the iniquity of the fathers on the children to the third and fourth generation of those who hate me, but showing steadfast love to thousands of those who love me and keep my commandments.

(Deuteronomy 5:8-10)

Q 50 What is required in the second commandment?

A The second commandment requireth the receiving, observing, and keeping pure and entire, all such religious worship and ordinances as God hath appointed in his Word (127)

(127) "Everything that I command you, you shall be careful to do. You shall not add to it or take from it.

(Deuteronomy 12:32)

teaching them to observe all that I have commanded you. And behold, I am with you always, to the end of the age."

(Matthew 28:20)

Q 51 What is forbidden in the second commandment?

A The second commandment forbiddeth the worshiping of God by images,[128] **or any other way not appointed in his Word** [129]

[128] "Therefore watch yourselves very carefully. Since you saw no form on the day that the LORD spoke to you at Horeb out of the midst of the fire, beware lest you act corruptly by making a carved image for yourselves, in the form of any figure, the likeness of male or female, the likeness of any animal that is on the earth, the likeness of any winged bird that flies in the air, the likeness of anything that creeps on the ground, the likeness of any fish that is in the water under the earth. And beware lest you raise your eyes to heaven, and when you see the sun and the moon and the stars, all the host of heaven, you be drawn away and bow down to them and serve them, things that the LORD your God has allotted to all the peoples under the whole heaven.

(Deuteronomy 4:15-19)

Claiming to be wise, they became fools, and exchanged the glory of the immortal God for images resembling mortal man and birds and animals and creeping things.

(Romans 1:22-23)

[129] Now Nadab and Abihu, the sons of Aaron, each took his censer and put fire in it and laid incense on it and offered unauthorized fire before the LORD, which he had not commanded them. And fire came out from before the LORD and consumed them, and they died before the LORD.

(Leviticus 10:1-2)

Because the people have forsaken me and have profaned this place by making offerings in it to other gods whom neither they nor their fathers nor the kings of Judah have known; and because they have filled this place with the blood of innocents, and have built the high places of Baal to burn their sons in the fire as burnt offerings to Baal, which I did not command or decree, nor did it come into my mind--

(Jeremiah 19:4-5)

Let no one disqualify you, insisting on asceticism and worship of angels, going on in detail about visions, puffed up without reason by his sensuous mind, and not holding fast to the Head, from whom the whole body, nourished and knit together through its joints and ligaments, grows with a growth that is from God. If with Christ you died to the elemental spirits of the world, why, as if you were still alive in the world, do you submit to regulations-- "Do not handle, Do not taste, Do not touch" (referring to things that all perish as they are used)-- according to human precepts and teachings? These have indeed an appearance of wisdom in promoting self-made religion and asceticism and severity to the body, but they are of no value in stopping the indulgence of the flesh.

(Colossians 2:18-23)

Q 52 What are the reasons annexed to the second commandment?

A The reasons annexed to the second commandment are, God's sovereignty over us,[130] **his propriety in us,**[131] **and the zeal he hath to his own worship** [132]

[130] Let us come into his presence with thanksgiving; let us make a joyful noise to him with songs of praise! For the LORD is a great God, and a great King above all gods.

(Psalms 95:2-3)

Oh come, let us worship and bow down; let us kneel before the LORD, our Maker! For he is our God, and we are the people of his pasture, and the sheep of his hand. Today, if you hear his voice,

(Psalms 95:6-7)

Worship the LORD in the splendor of holiness; tremble before him, all the earth! Say among the nations, "The LORD reigns! Yes, the world is established; it shall never be moved; he will judge the peoples with equity."

(Psalms 96:9-10)

[131] Now therefore, if you will indeed obey my voice and keep my covenant, you shall be my treasured possession among all peoples, for all the earth is mine;

(Exodus 19:5)

and the king will desire your beauty. Since he is your lord, bow to him.

(Psalms 45:11)

For your Maker is your husband, the LORD of hosts is his name; and the Holy One of Israel is your Redeemer, the God of the whole earth he is called.

(Isaiah 54:5)

[132] (for you shall worship no other god, for the LORD, whose name is Jealous, is a jealous God),

(Exodus 34:14)

Shall we provoke the Lord to jealousy? Are we stronger than he?

(1 Corinthians 10:22)

:

Q 53 Which is the third commandment?

A The third commandment is, Thou shalt not take the name of the Lord thy God in vain: for the Lord will not hold him guiltless that taketh his name in vain (133)

(133)"You shall not take the name of the LORD your God in vain, for the LORD will not hold him guiltless who takes his name in vain.

(Exodus 20:7)

'"You shall not take the name of the LORD your God in vain, for the LORD will not hold him guiltless who takes his name in vain.

(Deuteronomy 5:11)

Q 54 What is required in the third commandment?

A The third commandment requireth the holy and reverent use of God's names, titles,[134] attributes,[135] ordinances,[136] Word,[137] and works [138]

[134] You shall fear the LORD your God. You shall serve him and hold fast to him, and by his name you shall swear.

(Deuteronomy 10:20)

Ascribe to the LORD the glory due his name; worship the LORD in the splendor of holiness.

(Psalms 29:2)

Pray then like this: "Our Father in heaven, hallowed be your name.

(Matthew 6:9)

[135] Therefore David blessed the LORD in the presence of all the assembly. And David said: "Blessed are you, O LORD, the God of Israel our father, forever and ever. Yours, O LORD, is the greatness and the power and the glory and the victory and the majesty, for all that is in the heavens and in the earth is yours. Yours is the kingdom, O LORD, and you are exalted as head above all. Both riches and honor come from you, and you rule over all. In your hand are power and might, and in your hand it is to make great and to give strength to all. And now we thank you, our God, and praise your glorious name.

(1 Chronicles 29:10-13)

And they sing the song of Moses, the servant of God, and the song of the Lamb, saying, "Great and amazing are your deeds, O Lord God the Almighty! Just and true are your ways, O King of the nations! Who will not fear, O Lord, and glorify your name? For you alone are holy. All nations will come and worship you, for your righteous acts have been revealed."

(Revelation 15:3-4)

(136) And they devoted themselves to the apostles' teaching and the fellowship, to the breaking of bread and the prayers.

(Acts 2:42)

Whoever, therefore, eats the bread or drinks the cup of the Lord in an unworthy manner will be guilty concerning the body and blood of the Lord. Let a person examine himself, then, and so eat of the bread and drink of the cup.

(1 Corinthians 11:27-28)

(137) I bow down toward your holy temple and give thanks to your name for your steadfast love and your faithfulness, for you have exalted above all things your name and your word.

(Psalms 138:2)

I warn everyone who hears the words of the prophecy of this book: if anyone adds to them, God will add to him the plagues described in this book, and if anyone takes away from the words of the book of this prophecy, God will take away his share in the tree of life and in the holy city, which are described in this book.

(Revelation 22:18-19)

(138) Let them thank the LORD for his steadfast love, for his wondrous works to the children of man! And let them offer sacrifices of thanksgiving, and tell of his deeds in songs of joy!

(Psalms 107:21-22)

"Worthy are you, our Lord and God, to receive glory and honor and power, for you created all things, and by your will they existed and were created."

(Revelation 4:11)

Q 55 What is forbidden in the third commandment?

A The third commandment forbiddeth all profaning or abusing of anything whereby God maketh himself known (139)

(139)You shall not swear by my name falsely, and so profane the name of your God: I am the LORD.

(Leviticus 19:12)

"Again you have heard that it was said to those of old, 'You shall not swear falsely, but shall perform to the Lord what you have sworn.' But I say to you, Do not take an oath at all, either by heaven, for it is the throne of God, or by the earth, for it is his footstool, or by Jerusalem, for it is the city of the great King. And do not take an oath by your head, for you cannot make one hair white or black. Let what you say be simply 'Yes' or 'No'; anything more than this comes from evil.

(Matthew 5:33-37)

But above all, my brothers, do not swear, either by heaven or by earth or by any other oath, but let your "yes" be yes and your "no" be no, so that you may not fall under condemnation.

(James 5:12)

Q 56 What is the reason annexed to the third commandment?

A **The reason annexed to the third commandment is, that however the breakers of this commandment may escape punishment from men, yet the Lord our God will not suffer them to escape his righteous judgment** (140)

(140) "If you are not careful to do all the words of this law that are written in this book, that you may fear this glorious and awesome name, the LORD your God, then the LORD will bring on you and your offspring extraordinary afflictions, afflictions severe and lasting, and sicknesses grievous and lasting.

(Deuteronomy 28:58-59)

And I declare to him that I am about to punish his house forever, for the iniquity that he knew, because his sons were blaspheming God, and he did not restrain them.

(1 Samuel 3:13)

And the ark of God was captured, and the two sons of Eli, Hophni and Phinehas, died.

(1 Samuel 4:11)

Q 57 Which is the fourth commandment?

A The fourth commandment is, Remember the sabbath day to keep it holy Six days shalt thou labor, and do all thy work: but the seventh day is the sabbath of the Lord thy God: in it thou shalt not do any work, thou, nor thy son, nor thy daughter, thy manservant, nor thy maidservant, nor thy cattle, nor thy stranger that is within thy gates: For in six days the Lord made heaven and earth, the sea, and all that in them is, and rested the seventh day: wherefore the Lord blessed the sabbath day, and hallowed it (141)

(141) "Remember the Sabbath day, to keep it holy. Six days you shall labor, and do all your work, but the seventh day is a Sabbath to the LORD your God. On it you shall not do any work, you, or your son, or your daughter, your male servant, or your female servant, or your livestock, or the sojourner who is within your gates. For in six days the LORD made heaven and earth, the sea, and all that is in them, and rested on the seventh day. Therefore the LORD blessed the Sabbath day and made it holy.

(Exodus 20:8-11)

"'Observe the Sabbath day, to keep it holy, as the LORD your God commanded you. Six days you shall labor and do all your work, but the seventh day is a Sabbath to the LORD your God. On it you shall not do any work, you or your son or your daughter or your male servant or your female servant, or your ox or your donkey or any of your livestock, or the sojourner who is within your gates, that your male servant and your female servant may rest as well as you. You shall remember that you were a slave in the land of Egypt, and the LORD your God brought you out from there with a mighty hand and an outstretched arm. Therefore the LORD your God commanded you to keep the Sabbath day.

(Deuteronomy 5:12-15)

Q 58 What is required in the fourth commandment?

A The fourth commandment requireth the keeping holy to God such set times as he hath appointed in his Word; expressly one whole day in seven, to be a holy sabbath to himself (142)

(142) "You are to speak to the people of Israel and say, 'Above all you shall keep my Sabbaths, for this is a sign between me and you throughout your generations, that you may know that I, the LORD, sanctify you.

(Exodus 31:13)

Therefore the people of Israel shall keep the Sabbath, observing the Sabbath throughout their generations, as a covenant forever. It is a sign forever between me and the people of Israel that in six days the LORD made heaven and earth, and on the seventh day he rested and was refreshed.'"

(Exodus 31:16-17)

Q 59 Which day of the seven hath God appointed to be the weekly sabbath?

A From the beginning of the world to the resurrection of Christ, God appointed the seventh day of the week to be the weekly sabbath;(143) and the first day of the week ever since, to continue to the end of the world, which is the Christian sabbath (144)

(143) And on the seventh day God finished his work that he had done, and he rested on the seventh day from all his work that he had done. So God blessed the seventh day and made it holy, because on it God rested from all his work that he had done in creation.

(Genesis 2:2-3)

For in six days the LORD made heaven and earth, the sea, and all that is in them, and rested on the seventh day. Therefore the LORD blessed the Sabbath day and made it holy.

(Exodus 20:11)

(144) And he said to them, "The Sabbath was made for man, not man for the Sabbath. So the Son of Man is lord even of the Sabbath."

(Mark 2:27-28)

On the first day of the week, when we were gathered together to break bread, Paul talked with them, intending to depart on the next day, and he prolonged his speech until midnight.

(Acts 20:7)

On the first day of every week, each of you is to put something aside and store it up, as he may prosper, so that there will be no collecting when I come.

(1 Corinthians 16:2)

I was in the Spirit on the Lord's day, and I heard behind me a loud voice like a trumpet

(Revelation 1:10)

Q 60 How is the sabbath to be sanctified?

A The sabbath is to be sanctified by a holy resting all that day, even from such worldly employments and recreations as are lawful on other days;[145] and spending the whole time in the public and private exercises of God's worship,[146] except so much as is to be taken up in the works of necessity and mercy [147]

[145] but the seventh day is a Sabbath to the LORD your God. On it you shall not do any work, you, or your son, or your daughter, your male servant, or your female servant, or your livestock, or the sojourner who is within your gates.

(Exodus 20:10)

In those days I saw in Judah people treading winepresses on the Sabbath, and bringing in heaps of grain and loading them on donkeys, and also wine, grapes, figs, and all kinds of loads, which they brought into Jerusalem on the Sabbath day. And I warned them on the day when they sold food. Tyrians also, who lived in the city, brought in fish and all kinds of goods and sold them on the Sabbath to the people of Judah, in Jerusalem itself! Then I confronted the nobles of Judah and said to them, "What is this evil thing that you are doing, profaning the Sabbath day? Did not your fathers act in this way, and did not our God bring all this disaster on us and on this city? Now you are bringing more wrath on Israel by profaning the Sabbath." As soon as it began to grow dark at the gates of Jerusalem before the Sabbath, I commanded that the doors should be shut and gave orders that they should not be opened until after the Sabbath. And I stationed some of my servants at the gates, that no load might be brought in on the Sabbath day. Then the merchants and sellers of all kinds of wares lodged outside Jerusalem once or twice. But I warned them and said to them, "Why do you lodge outside the wall? If you do so again, I will lay hands on you." From that time on they did not come on the Sabbath. Then I commanded the Levites that they should purify themselves and come and guard the gates, to keep the Sabbath day holy. Remember this also in my favor, O my God, and spare me according to the greatness of your steadfast love.

(Nehemiah 13:15-22)

"If you turn back your foot from the Sabbath, from doing your pleasure on my holy day, and call the Sabbath a delight and the holy day of the LORD honorable; if you honor it, not going your own ways, or seeking your own pleasure, or talking idly; then you shall take delight in the LORD, and I will make you ride on the heights of the earth; I will feed you with the heritage of Jacob your father, for the mouth of the LORD has spoken."

(Isaiah 58:13-14)

(146) "Remember the Sabbath day, to keep it holy.

(Exodus 20:8)

"Six days shall work be done, but on the seventh day is a Sabbath of solemn rest, a holy convocation. You shall do no work. It is a Sabbath to the LORD in all your dwelling places.

(Leviticus 23:3)

And he came to Nazareth, where he had been brought up. And as was his custom, he went to the synagogue on the Sabbath day, and he stood up to read.

(Luke 4:16)

On the first day of the week, when we were gathered together to break bread, Paul talked with them, intending to depart on the next day, and he prolonged his speech until midnight.

(Acts 20:7)

At that time Jesus went through the grainfields on the Sabbath. His disciples were hungry, and they began to pluck heads of grain and to eat. But when the Pharisees saw it, they said to him, "Look, your disciples are doing what is not lawful to do on the Sabbath." He said to them, "Have you not read what David did when he was hungry, and those who were with him: how he entered the house of God and ate the bread of the Presence, which it was not lawful for him to eat nor for those who were with him, but only for the priests? Or have you not read in the Law how on the Sabbath the priests in the temple profane the Sabbath and are guiltless? I tell you, something greater than the temple is here. And if you had known what this means, 'I desire mercy, and not sacrifice,' you would not have condemned the guiltless. For the Son of Man is lord of the Sabbath." He went on from there and entered their synagogue. And a man was there with a withered hand. And they asked him, "Is it lawful to heal on the Sabbath?"--so that they might accuse him. He said to them, "Which one of you who has a sheep, if it falls into a pit on the Sabbath, will not take hold of it and lift it out? Of how much more value is a man than a sheep! So it is lawful to do good on the Sabbath." Then he said to the man, "Stretch out your hand." And the man stretched it out, and it was restored, healthy like the other.

(Matthew 12:1-13)

Q 61 What is forbidden in the fourth commandment?

A The fourth commandment forbiddeth the omission, or careless performance, of the duties required, and the profaning the day by idleness, or doing that which is in itself sinful, or by unnecessary thoughts, words, or works, about our worldly employments or recreations (148)

(148) In those days I saw in Judah people treading winepresses on the Sabbath, and bringing in heaps of grain and loading them on donkeys, and also wine, grapes, figs, and all kinds of loads, which they brought into Jerusalem on the Sabbath day. And I warned them on the day when they sold food. Tyrians also, who lived in the city, brought in fish and all kinds of goods and sold them on the Sabbath to the people of Judah, in Jerusalem itself! Then I confronted the nobles of Judah and said to them, "What is this evil thing that you are doing, profaning the Sabbath day? Did not your fathers act in this way, and did not our God bring all this disaster on us and on this city? Now you are bringing more wrath on Israel by profaning the Sabbath." As soon as it began to grow dark at the gates of Jerusalem before the Sabbath, I commanded that the doors should be shut and gave orders that they should not be opened until after the Sabbath. And I stationed some of my servants at the gates, that no load might be brought in on the Sabbath day. Then the merchants and sellers of all kinds of wares lodged outside Jerusalem once or twice. But I warned them and said to them, "Why do you lodge outside the wall? If you do so again, I will lay hands on you." From that time on they did not come on the Sabbath. Then I commanded the Levites that they should purify themselves and come and guard the gates, to keep the Sabbath day holy. Remember this also in my favor, O my God, and spare me according to the greatness of your steadfast love.

(Nehemiah 13:15-22)

"If you turn back your foot from the Sabbath, from doing your pleasure on my holy day, and call the Sabbath a delight and the holy day of the LORD honorable; if you honor it, not going your own ways, or seeking your own pleasure, or talking idly; then you shall take delight in the LORD, and I will make you ride on the heights of the earth; I will feed you with the heritage of Jacob your father, for the mouth of the LORD has spoken."

(Isaiah 58:13-14)

Hear this, you who trample on the needy and bring the poor of the land to an end, saying, "When will the new moon be over, that we may sell grain? And the Sabbath, that we may offer wheat for sale, that we may make the ephah small and the shekel great and deal deceitfully with false balances, that we may buy the poor for silver and the needy for a pair of sandals and sell the chaff of the wheat?"

(Amos 8:4-6)

Q 62. What are the reasons annexed to the fourth commandment?

A The reasons annexed to the fourth commandment are, God's allowing us six days of the week for our own employments,(149) his challenging a special propriety in the seventh, his own example, and his blessing the Sabbath-day.(150)

(149) Six days you shall labor, and do all your work,

(Exodus 20:9)

Six days shall work be done, but the seventh day is a Sabbath of solemn rest, holy to the LORD. Whoever does any work on the Sabbath day shall be put to death.

(Exodus 31:15)

"Six days shall work be done, but on the seventh day is a Sabbath of solemn rest, a holy convocation. You shall do no work. It is a Sabbath to the LORD in all your dwelling places.

(Leviticus 23:3)

(150) "Six days shall work be done, but on the seventh day is a Sabbath of solemn rest, a holy convocation. You shall do no work. It is a Sabbath to the LORD in all your dwelling places.

(Leviticus 23:3)

And on the seventh day God finished his work that he had done, and he rested on the seventh day from all his work that he had done. So God blessed the seventh day and made it holy, because on it God rested from all his work that he had done in creation.

(Genesis 2:2-3)

For in six days the LORD made heaven and earth, the sea, and all that is in them, and rested on the seventh day. Therefore the LORD blessed the Sabbath day and made it holy.

(Exodus 20:11)

It is a sign forever between me and the people of Israel that in six days the LORD made heaven and earth, and on the seventh day he rested and was refreshed."'

(Exodus 31:17)

Q 63 Which is the fifth commandment?

A The fifth commandment is, Honor thy father and thy mother: that thy days may be long upon the land which the Lord thy God giveth thee (151)

(151) "Honor your father and your mother, that your days may be long in the land that the LORD your God is giving you.

(Exodus 20:12)

"'Honor your father and your mother, as the LORD your God commanded you, that your days may be long, and that it may go well with you in the land that the LORD your God is giving you.

(Deuteronomy 5:16)

Q 64 What is required in the fifth commandment?

A The fifth commandment requireth the preserving the honor, and performing the duties, belonging to everyone in their several places and relations, as superiors, inferiors, or equals (152)

(152) Let every person be subject to the governing authorities. For there is no authority except from God, and those that exist have been instituted by God.

(Romans 13:1)

Pay to all what is owed to them: taxes to whom taxes are owed, revenue to whom revenue is owed, respect to whom respect is owed, honor to whom honor is owed.

(Romans 13:7)

submitting to one another out of reverence for Christ. Wives, submit to your own husbands, as to the Lord.

(Ephesians 5:21-22)

Now as the church submits to Christ, so also wives should submit in everything to their husbands.

(Ephesians 5:24)

Children, obey your parents in the Lord, for this is right.

(Ephesians 6:1)

Fathers, do not provoke your children to anger, but bring them up in the discipline and instruction of the Lord. Slaves, obey your earthly masters with fear and trembling, with a sincere heart, as you would Christ,

(Ephesians 6:4-5)

Masters, do the same to them, and stop your threatening, knowing that he who is both their Master and yours is in heaven, and that there is no partiality with him.

(Ephesians 6:9)

Honor everyone. Love the brotherhood. Fear God. Honor the emperor.

(1 Peter 2:17)

Q 65 What is forbidden in the fifth commandment?

A The fifth commandment forbiddeth the neglecting of, or doing anything against, the honor and duty which belongeth to everyone in their several places and relations (153)

(153) For God commanded, 'Honor your father and your mother,' and, 'Whoever reviles father or mother must surely die.' But you say, 'If anyone tells his father or his mother, "What you would have gained from me is given to God," he need not honor his father.' So for the sake of your tradition you have made void the word of God.

(Matthew 15:4-6)

Owe no one anything, except to love each other, for the one who loves another has fulfilled the law.

(Romans 13:8)

Q 66 What is the reason annexed to the fifth commandment?

A The reason annexed to the fifth commandment is, a promise of long life and prosperity (as far as it shall serve for God's glory and their own good) to all such as keep this commandment (154)

(154) "Honor your father and your mother, that your days may be long in the land that the LORD your God is giving you.

(Exodus 20:12)

"'Honor your father and your mother, as the LORD your God commanded you, that your days may be long, and that it may go well with you in the land that the LORD your God is giving you.

(Deuteronomy 5:16)

"Honor your father and mother" (this is the first commandment with a promise), "that it may go well with you and that you may live long in the land."

(Ephesians 6:2-3)

Q 67 Which is the sixth commandment?

A The sixth commandment is, Thou shalt not kill [155]

[155] "You shall not murder.

(Exodus 20:13)

"'You shall not murder.

(Deuteronomy 5:17)

Q 68 What is required in the sixth commandment?

A The sixth commandment requireth all lawful endeavors to preserve our own life, and the life of others (156)

(156) In the same way husbands should love their wives as their own bodies. He who loves his wife loves himself. For no one ever hated his own flesh, but nourishes and cherishes it, just as Christ does the church,

(Ephesians 5:28-29)

Q 69 What is forbidden in the sixth commandment?

A **The sixth commandment forbiddeth the taking away of our own life, or the life of our neighbor, unjustly, or whatsoever tendeth thereunto** (157)

(157) "Whoever sheds the blood of man, by man shall his blood be shed, for God made man in his own image.

(Genesis 9:6)

But I say to you that everyone who is angry with his brother will be liable to judgment; whoever insults his brother will be liable to the council; and whoever says, 'You fool!' will be liable to the hell of fire.

(Matthew 5:22)

Everyone who hates his brother is a murderer, and you know that no murderer has eternal life abiding in him.

(1 John 3:15)

Q 70 Which is the seventh commandment?

A The seventh commandment is, Thou shalt not commit adultery (158)

(158) "You shall not commit adultery.

(Exodus 20:14)

"'And you shall not commit adultery.

(Deuteronomy 5:18)

Q 71 What is required in the seventh commandment?

A The seventh commandment requireth the preservation of our own and our neighbor's chastity, in heart, speech, and behavior (159)

(159) But because of the temptation to sexual immorality, each man should have his own wife and each woman her own husband. The husband should give to his wife her conjugal rights, and likewise the wife to her husband.

(1 Corinthians 7:2-3)

For this is the will of God, your sanctification: that you abstain from sexual immorality; that each one of you know how to control his own body in holiness and honor, not in the passion of lust like the Gentiles who do not know God;

(1 Thessalonians 4:3-5)

Q 72 What is forbidden in the seventh commandment?

A The seventh commandment forbiddeth all unchaste thoughts, words, and actions (160)

(160) But I say to you that everyone who looks at a woman with lustful intent has already committed adultery with her in his heart.

(Matthew 5:28)

But sexual immorality and all impurity or covetousness must not even be named among you, as is proper among saints. Let there be no filthiness nor foolish talk nor crude joking, which are out of place, but instead let there be thanksgiving.

(Ephesians 5:3-4)

Q 73 Which is the eighth commandment?

A The eighth commandment is, Thou shalt not steal [161]

[161] "You shall not steal.

(Exodus 20:15)

"'And you shall not steal.

(Deuteronomy 5:19)

Q 74 What is required in the eighth commandment?

A The eighth commandment requireth the lawful procuring and furthering the wealth and outward estate of ourselves and others (162)

(162) "If your brother becomes poor and cannot maintain himself with you, you shall support him as though he were a stranger and a sojourner, and he shall live with you.

(Leviticus 25:35)

but rather let him labor, doing honest work with his own hands, so that he may have something to share with anyone in need.

(Ephesians 4:28)

Let each of you look not only to his own interests, but also to the interests of others.

(Philippians 2:4)

Q 75 What is forbidden in the eighth commandment?

A The eighth commandment forbiddeth whatsoever doth, or may, unjustly hinder our own, or our neighbor's wealth or outward estate (163)

(163) Whoever works his land will have plenty of bread, but he who follows worthless pursuits will have plenty of poverty. A faithful man will abound with blessings, but whoever hastens to be rich will not go unpunished. To show partiality is not good, but for a piece of bread a man will do wrong. A stingy man hastens after wealth and does not know that poverty will come upon him. Whoever rebukes a man will afterward find more favor than he who flatters with his tongue. Whoever robs his father or his mother and says, "That is no transgression," is a companion to a man who destroys. A greedy man stirs up strife, but the one who trusts in the LORD will be enriched. Whoever trusts in his own mind is a fool, but he who walks in wisdom will be delivered. Whoever gives to the poor will not want, but he who hides his eyes will get many a curse.

(Proverbs 28:19-27)

but rather let him labor, doing honest work with his own hands, so that he may have something to share with anyone in need.

(Ephesians 4:28)

For even when we were with you, we would give you this command: If anyone is not willing to work, let him not eat.

(2 Thessalonians 3:10)

But if anyone does not provide for his relatives, and especially for members of his household, he has denied the faith and is worse than an unbeliever.

(1 Timothy 5:8)

Q 76 Which is the ninth commandment?

A The ninth commandment is, Thou shalt not bear false witness against thy neighbor (164)

(164) "You shall not bear false witness against your neighbor.

(Exodus 20:16)

"'And you shall not bear false witness against your neighbor.

(Deuteronomy 5:20)

Q 77 What is required in the ninth commandment?

A The ninth commandment requireth the maintaining and promoting of truth between man and man, and of our own and our neighbor's good name,[165] especially in witness-bearing [166]

[165] These are the things that you shall do: Speak the truth to one another; render in your gates judgments that are true and make for peace;

(Zechariah 8:16)

But Paul said, "I am standing before Caesar's tribunal, where I ought to be tried. To the Jews I have done no wrong, as you yourself know very well.

(Acts 25:10)

Beloved, I pray that all may go well with you and that you may be in good health, as it goes well with your soul.

(3 John 1:2)

[166] A faithful witness does not lie, but a false witness breathes out lies.

(Proverbs 14:5)

A truthful witness saves lives, but one who breathes out lies is deceitful.

(Proverbs 14:25)

Q 78 What is forbidden in the ninth commandment?

A The ninth commandment forbiddeth whatsoever is prejudicial to truth, or injurious to our own, or our neighbor's, good name (167)

(167) You shall not go around as a slanderer among your people, and you shall not stand up against the life of your neighbor: I am the LORD.

(Leviticus 19:16)

who does not slander with his tongue and does no evil to his neighbor, nor takes up a reproach against his friend;

(Psalms 15:3)

There are six things that the LORD hates, seven that are an abomination to him: haughty eyes, a lying tongue, and hands that shed innocent blood, a heart that devises wicked plans, feet that make haste to run to evil, a false witness who breathes out lies, and one who sows discord among brothers.

(Proverbs 6:16-19)

Soldiers also asked him, "And we, what shall we do?" And he said to them, "Do not extort money from anyone by threats or by false accusation, and be content with your wages."

(Luke 3:14)

Q 79 Which is the tenth commandment?

A The tenth commandment is, Thou shalt not covet thy neighbor's house, thou shalt not covet thy neighbor's wife, nor his manservant, nor his maidservant, nor his ox, nor his ass, nor anything that is thy neighbor's (168)

(168) "You shall not covet your neighbor's house; you shall not covet your neighbor's wife, or his male servant, or his female servant, or his ox, or his donkey, or anything that is your neighbor's."

(Exodus 20:17)

"'And you shall not covet your neighbor's wife. And you shall not desire your neighbor's house, his field, or his male servant, or his female servant, his ox, or his donkey, or anything that is your neighbor's.'

(Deuteronomy 5:21)

Q 80 What is required in the tenth commandment?

A The tenth commandment requireth full contentment with our own condition,(169) with a right and charitable frame of spirit toward our neighbor, and all that is his (170)

(169) Of David, when he changed his behavior before Abimelech, so that he drove him out, and he went away. I will bless the LORD at all times; his praise shall continually be in my mouth.

(Psalms 34:1)

Not that I am speaking of being in need, for I have learned in whatever situation I am to be content.

(Philippians 4:11)

Now there is great gain in godliness with contentment,

(1 Timothy 6:6)

Keep your life free from love of money, and be content with what you have, for he has said, "I will never leave you nor forsake you."

(Hebrews 13:5)

(170) And when he comes home, he calls together his friends and his neighbors, saying to them, 'Rejoice with me, for I have found my sheep that was lost.'

(Luke 15:6)

And when she has found it, she calls together her friends and neighbors, saying, 'Rejoice with me, for I have found the coin that I had lost.'

(Luke 15:9)

And he said, "There was a man who had two sons. And the younger of them said to his father, 'Father, give me the share of property that is coming to me.' And he divided his property between them. Not many days later, the younger son gathered all he had and took a journey into a far country, and there he squandered his property in reckless living. And when he had spent everything, a severe famine arose in that country, and he began to be in need. So he went and hired himself out to one of the citizens of that country, who sent him into his fields to feed pigs. And he was longing to be fed with the pods that the pigs ate, and no one gave him anything. "But when he came to himself, he said, 'How many of my father's hired servants have more than enough bread, but I perish here with hunger! I will arise and go to my father, and I will say to him, "Father, I have sinned against heaven and before you. I am no longer worthy to be called your son. Treat me as one of your hired servants."' And he arose and came to his father. But while he was still a long way off, his father saw him and felt compassion, and ran and embraced him and kissed him. And the son said to him, 'Father, I have sinned against heaven and before you. I am no longer worthy to be called your son.' But the father said to his servants, 'Bring quickly the best robe, and put it on him, and put a ring on his hand, and shoes on his feet. And bring the fattened calf and kill it, and let us eat and celebrate. For this my son was dead, and is alive again; he was lost, and is found.' And they began to celebrate. "Now his older son was in the field, and as he came and drew near to the house, he heard music and dancing. And he called one of the servants and asked what these things meant. And he said to him, 'Your brother has come, and your father has killed the fattened calf, because he has received him back safe and sound.' But he was angry and refused to go in. His father came out and entreated him, but he answered his father, 'Look, these many years I have served you, and I never disobeyed your command, yet you never gave me a young goat, that I might celebrate with my friends. But when this son of yours came, who has devoured your property with prostitutes, you killed the fattened calf for him!' And he said to him, 'Son, you are always with me, and all that is mine is yours. It was fitting to celebrate and be glad, for this your brother was dead, and is alive; he was lost, and is found.'"

(Luke 15:11-32)

Rejoice with those who rejoice, weep with those who weep.

(Romans 12:15)

Let each of you look not only to his own interests, but also to the interests of others.

(Philippians 2:4)

Q 81 What is forbidden in the tenth commandment?

A The tenth commandment forbiddeth all discontentment with our own estate,[171] **envying or grieving at the good of our neighbor, and all inordinate motions and affections to anything that is his** [172]

[171] nor grumble, as some of them did and were destroyed by the Destroyer.

(1 Corinthians 10:10)

But if you have bitter jealousy and selfish ambition in your hearts, do not boast and be false to the truth.

(James 3:14)

[172] Let us not become conceited, provoking one another, envying one another.

(Galatians 5:26)

Put to death therefore what is earthly in you: sexual immorality, impurity, passion, evil desire, and covetousness, which is idolatry.

(Colossians 3:5)

Q 82 Is any man able perfectly to keep the commandments of God?

A No mere man, since the fall, is able in this life perfectly to keep the commandments of God, but doth daily break them in thought, word, and deed (173)

(173) And when the LORD smelled the pleasing aroma, the LORD said in his heart, "I will never again curse the ground because of man, for the intention of man's heart is evil from his youth. Neither will I ever again strike down every living creature as I have done.

(Genesis 8:21)

What then? Are we Jews any better off? No, not at all. For we have already charged that all, both Jews and Greeks, are under sin, as it is written: "None is righteous, no, not one; no one understands; no one seeks for God. All have turned aside; together they have become worthless; no one does good, not even one." "Their throat is an open grave; they use their tongues to deceive." "The venom of asps is under their lips." "Their mouth is full of curses and bitterness." "Their feet are swift to shed blood; in their paths are ruin and misery, and the way of peace they have not known." "There is no fear of God before their eyes." Now we know that whatever the law says it speaks to those who are under the law, so that every mouth may be stopped, and the whole world may be held accountable to God. For by works of the law no human being will be justified in his sight, since through the law comes knowledge of sin. But now the righteousness of God has been manifested apart from the law, although the Law and the Prophets bear witness to it-- the righteousness of God through faith in Jesus Christ for all who believe. For there is no distinction: for all have sinned and fall short of the glory of God,

(Romans 3:9-23)

Q 83 Are all transgressions of the law equally heinous?

A Some sins in themselves, and by reason of several aggravations, are more heinous in the sight of God than others (174)

(174) And he said to me, "Son of man, do you see what they are doing, the great abominations that the house of Israel are committing here, to drive me far from my sanctuary? But you will see still greater abominations."

(Ezekiel 8:6)

He said also to me, "You will see still greater abominations that they commit."

(Ezekiel 8:13)

Then he said to me, "Have you seen this, O son of man? You will see still greater abominations than these."

(Ezekiel 8:15)

Then he began to denounce the cities where most of his mighty works had been done, because they did not repent. "Woe to you, Chorazin! Woe to you, Bethsaida! For if the mighty works done in you had been done in Tyre and Sidon, they would have repented long ago in sackcloth and ashes. But I tell you, it will be more bearable on the day of judgment for Tyre and Sidon than for you. And you, Capernaum, will you be exalted to heaven? You will be brought down to Hades. For if the mighty works done in you had been done in Sodom, it would have remained until this day. But I tell you that it will be more tolerable on the day of judgment for the land of Sodom than for you."

(Matthew 11:20-24)

Jesus answered him, "You would have no authority over me at all unless it had been given you from above. Therefore he who delivered me over to you has the greater sin."

(John 19:11)

Q 84 What doth every sin deserve?

A Every sin deserveth God's wrath and curse, both in this life, and that which is to come [175]

[175] "Then he will say to those on his left, 'Depart from me, you cursed, into the eternal fire prepared for the devil and his angels.

(Matthew 25:41)

For all who rely on works of the law are under a curse; for it is written, "Cursed be everyone who does not abide by all things written in the Book of the Law, and do them."

(Galatians 3:10)

Let no one deceive you with empty words, for because of these things the wrath of God comes upon the sons of disobedience.

(Ephesians 5:6)

For whoever keeps the whole law but fails in one point has become accountable for all of it.

(James 2:10)

Q 85 What doth God require of us, that we may escape his wrath and curse, due to us for sin?

A To escape the wrath and curse of God, due to us for sin, God requireth of us faith in Jesus Christ, repentance unto life,[176] with the diligent use of all the outward means whereby Christ communicateth to us the benefits of redemption [177]

[176] and saying, "The time is fulfilled, and the kingdom of God is at hand; repent and believe in the gospel."

(Mark 1:15)

testifying both to Jews and to Greeks of repentance toward God and of faith in our Lord Jesus Christ.

(Acts 20:21)

[177] And Peter said to them, "Repent and be baptized every one of you in the name of Jesus Christ for the forgiveness of your sins, and you will receive the gift of the Holy Spirit.

(Acts 2:38)

and when he had given thanks, he broke it, and said, "This is my body which is for you. Do this in remembrance of me." In the same way also he took the cup, after supper, saying, "This cup is the new covenant in my blood. Do this, as often as you drink it, in remembrance of me."

(1 Corinthians 11:24-25)

Let the word of Christ dwell in you richly, teaching and admonishing one another in all wisdom, singing psalms and hymns and spiritual songs, with thankfulness in your hearts to God.

(Colossians 3:16)

Q 86 What is faith in Jesus Christ?

A Faith in Jesus Christ is a saving grace,[178] **whereby we receive and rest upon him alone for salvation, as he is offered to us in the gospel** [179]

[178] For by grace you have been saved through faith. And this is not your own doing; it is the gift of God, not a result of works, so that no one may boast.

(Ephesians 2:8-9)

That is why it depends on faith, in order that the promise may rest on grace and be guaranteed to all his offspring--not only to the adherent of the law but also to the one who shares the faith of Abraham, who is the father of us all,

(Romans 4:16)

[179] Now Jesus did many other signs in the presence of the disciples, which are not written in this book; but these are written so that you may believe that Jesus is the Christ, the Son of God, and that by believing you may have life in his name.

(John 20:30-31)

We ourselves are Jews by birth and not Gentile sinners; yet we know that a person is not justified by works of the law but through faith in Jesus Christ, so we also have believed in Christ Jesus, in order to be justified by faith in Christ and not by works of the law, because by works of the law no one will be justified.

(Galatians 2:15-16)

For we are the circumcision, who worship by the Spirit of God and glory in Christ Jesus and put no confidence in the flesh-- though I myself have reason for confidence in the flesh also. If anyone else thinks he has reason for confidence in the flesh, I have more: circumcised on the eighth day, of the people of Israel, of the tribe of Benjamin, a Hebrew of Hebrews; as to the law, a Pharisee; as to zeal, a persecutor of the church; as to righteousness under the law, blameless. But whatever gain I had, I counted as loss for the sake of Christ. Indeed, I count everything as loss because of the surpassing worth of knowing Christ Jesus my Lord. For his sake I have suffered the loss of all things and count them as rubbish, in order that I may gain Christ and be found in him, not having a righteousness of my own that comes from the law, but that which comes through faith in Christ, the righteousness from God that depends on faith-- that I may know him and the power of his resurrection, and may share his sufferings, becoming like him in his death, that by any means possible I may attain the resurrection from the dead.

(Philippians 3:3-11)

Q 87 What is repentance unto life?

A **Repentance unto life is a saving grace,**[180] **whereby a sinner, out of a true sense of his sin, and apprehension of the mercy of God in Christ,**[181] **doth, with grief and hatred of his sin, turn from it unto God,**[182] **with full purpose of, and endeavor after, new obedience** [183]

[180] When they heard these things they fell silent. And they glorified God, saying, "Then to the Gentiles also God has granted repentance that leads to life."

(Acts 11:18)

correcting his opponents with gentleness. God may perhaps grant them repentance leading to a knowledge of the truth,

(2 Timothy 2:25)

To the choirmaster. A Psalm of David, when Nathan the prophet went to him, after he had gone in to Bathsheba. Have mercy on me, O God, according to your steadfast love; according to your abundant mercy blot out my transgressions. Wash me thoroughly from my iniquity, and cleanse me from my sin! For I know my transgressions, and my sin is ever before me. Against you, you only, have I sinned and done what is evil in your sight, so that you may be justified in your words and blameless in your judgment.

(Psalms 51:1-4)

and rend your hearts and not your garments." Return to the LORD your God, for he is gracious and merciful, slow to anger, and abounding in steadfast love; and he relents over disaster.

(Joel 2:13)

Just so, I tell you, there will be more joy in heaven over one sinner who repents than over ninety-nine righteous persons who need no repentance.

(Luke 15:7)

Now when they heard this they were cut to the heart, and said to Peter and the rest of the apostles, "Brothers, what shall we do?"

(Acts 2:37)

(182) I have heard Ephraim grieving, 'You have disciplined me, and I was disciplined, like an untrained calf; bring me back that I may be restored, for you are the LORD my God. For after I had turned away, I relented, and after I was instructed, I struck my thigh; I was ashamed, and I was confounded, because I bore the disgrace of my youth.'

(Jeremiah 31:18-19)

And he will turn many of the children of Israel to the Lord their God, and he will go before him in the spirit and power of Elijah, to turn the hearts of the fathers to the children, and the disobedient to the wisdom of the just, to make ready for the Lord a people prepared."

(Luke 1:16-17)

For they themselves report concerning us the kind of reception we had among you, and how you turned to God from idols to serve the living and true God,

(1 Thessalonians 1:9)

(183) if my people who are called by my name humble themselves, and pray and seek my face and turn from their wicked ways, then I will hear from heaven and will forgive their sin and heal their land.

(2 Chronicles 7:14)

The LORD is my portion; I promise to keep your words. I entreat your favor with all my heart; be gracious to me according to your promise. When I think on my ways, I turn my feet to your testimonies; I hasten and do not delay to keep your commandments. Though the cords of the wicked ensnare me, I do not forget your law. At midnight I rise to praise you, because of your righteous rules. I am a companion of all who fear you, of those who keep your precepts. The earth, O LORD, is full of your steadfast love; teach me your statutes!

(Psalms 119:57-64)

Bear fruit in keeping with repentance.

(Matthew 3:8)

For godly grief produces a repentance that leads to salvation without regret, whereas worldly grief produces death.

(2 Corinthians 7:10)

Q 88 What are the outward and ordinary means whereby Christ communicateth to us the benefits of redemption?

A The outward and ordinary means whereby Christ communicateth to us the benefits of redemption are, his ordinances, especially the Word, sacraments, and prayer; all which are made effectual to the elect for salvation (184)

(184) And Jesus came and said to them, "All authority in heaven and on earth has been given to me. Go therefore and make disciples of all nations, baptizing them in the name of the Father and of the Son and of the Holy Spirit, teaching them to observe all that I have commanded you. And behold, I am with you always, to the end of the age."

(Matthew 28:18-20)

So those who received his word were baptized, and there were added that day about three thousand souls. And they devoted themselves to the apostles' teaching and the fellowship, to the breaking of bread and the prayers.

(Acts 2:41-42)

Q 89 How is the Word made effectual to salvation?

A The Spirit of God maketh the reading, but especially the preaching, of the Word, an effectual means of convincing and converting sinners, and of building them up in holiness and comfort, through faith, unto salvation (185)

(185) They read from the book, from the Law of God, clearly, and they gave the sense, so that the people understood the reading. And Nehemiah, who was the governor, and Ezra the priest and scribe, and the Levites who taught the people said to all the people, "This day is holy to the LORD your God; do not mourn or weep." For all the people wept as they heard the words of the Law.

(Nehemiah 8:8-9)

And now I commend you to God and to the word of his grace, which is able to build you up and to give you the inheritance among all those who are sanctified.

(Acts 20:32)

How then will they call on him in whom they have not believed? And how are they to believe in him of whom they have never heard? And how are they to hear without someone preaching? And how are they to preach unless they are sent? As it is written, "How beautiful are the feet of those who preach the good news!" But they have not all obeyed the gospel. For Isaiah says, "Lord, who has believed what he has heard from us?" So faith comes from hearing, and hearing through the word of Christ.

(Romans 10:14-17)

and how from childhood you have been acquainted with the sacred writings, which are able to make you wise for salvation through faith in Christ Jesus. All Scripture is breathed out by God and profitable for teaching, for reproof, for correction, and for training in righteousness, that the man of God may be competent, equipped for every good work.

(2 Timothy 3:15-17)

Q 90 How is the Word to be read and heard, that it may become effectual to salvation?

A That the Word may become effectual to salvation, we must attend thereunto with diligence, preparation, and prayer;[186] receive it with faith and love, lay it up in our hearts, and practice it in our lives [187]

[186] "You shall not put the LORD your God to the test, as you tested him at Massah.

(Deuteronomy 6:16)

Open my eyes, that I may behold wondrous things out of your law.

(Psalms 119:18)

So put away all malice and all deceit and hypocrisy and envy and all slander. Like newborn infants, long for the pure spiritual milk, that by it you may grow up into salvation--

(1 Peter 2:1-2)

[187] I have stored up your word in my heart, that I might not sin against you.

(Psalms 119:11)

and with all wicked deception for those who are perishing, because they refused to love the truth and so be saved.

(2 Thessalonians 2:10)

For good news came to us just as to them, but the message they heard did not benefit them, because they were not united by faith with those who listened.

(Hebrews 4:2)

But be doers of the word, and not hearers only, deceiving yourselves. For if anyone is a hearer of the word and not a doer, he is like a man who looks intently at his natural face in a mirror. For he looks at himself and goes away and at once forgets what he was like. But the one who looks into the perfect law, the law of liberty, and perseveres, being no hearer who forgets but a doer who acts, he will be blessed in his doing.

(James 1:22-25)

Q 91. How do the sacraments become effectual means of salvation?

A The sacraments become effectual means of salvation, not from any virtue in them, or in him that doth administer them, but only by the blessing of Christ, and the working of his Spirit in them that by faith receive them.[188]

(188) So neither he who plants nor he who waters is anything, but only God who gives the growth.

(1 Corinthians 3:7)

What I mean is that each one of you says, "I follow Paul," or "I follow Apollos," or "I follow Cephas," or "I follow Christ." Is Christ divided? Was Paul crucified for you? Or were you baptized in the name of Paul? I thank God that I baptized none of you except Crispus and Gaius, so that no one may say that you were baptized in my name. (I did baptize also the household of Stephanas. Beyond that, I do not know whether I baptized anyone else.) For Christ did not send me to baptize but to preach the gospel, and not with words of eloquent wisdom, lest the cross of Christ be emptied of its power.

(1 Corinthians 1:12-17)

Q 92 What is a sacrament?

A A sacrament is a holy ordinance instituted by Christ;[189] **wherein, by sensible signs, Christ, and the benefits of the new covenant, are represented, sealed, and applied to believers** [190]

[189] Go therefore and make disciples of all nations, baptizing them in the name of the Father and of the Son and of the Holy Spirit,

(Matthew 28:19)

Now as they were eating, Jesus took bread, and after blessing it broke it and gave it to the disciples, and said, "Take, eat; this is my body." And he took a cup, and when he had given thanks he gave it to them, saying, "Drink of it, all of you, for this is my blood of the covenant, which is poured out for many for the forgiveness of sins.

(Matthew 26:26-28)

And as they were eating, he took bread, and after blessing it broke it and gave it to them, and said, "Take; this is my body." And he took a cup, and when he had given thanks he gave it to them, and they all drank of it. And he said to them, "This is my blood of the covenant, which is poured out for many. Truly, I say to you, I will not drink again of the fruit of the vine until that day when I drink it new in the kingdom of God."

(Mark 14:22-25)

And he took bread, and when he had given thanks, he broke it and gave it to them, saying, "This is my body, which is given for you. Do this in remembrance of me." And likewise the cup after they had eaten, saying, "This cup that is poured out for you is the new covenant in my blood.

(Luke 22:19-20)

For Jews demand signs and Greeks seek wisdom, but we preach Christ crucified, a stumbling block to Jews and folly to Gentiles, but to those who are called, both Jews and Greeks, Christ the power of God and the wisdom of God. For the foolishness of God is wiser than men, and the weakness of God is stronger than men. For consider your calling, brothers: not many of you were wise according to worldly standards, not many were powerful, not many were of noble birth.

(1 Corinthians 1:22-26)

[190] For as many of you as were baptized into Christ have put on Christ.

(Galatians 3:27)

The cup of blessing that we bless, is it not a participation in the blood of Christ? The bread that we break, is it not a participation in the body of Christ? Because there is one bread, we who are many are one body, for we all partake of the one bread.

(1 Corinthians 10:16-17)

Q 93 Which are the sacraments of the New Testament?

A The sacraments of the New Testament are, baptism,[191] and the Lord's Supper [192]

[191] Go therefore and make disciples of all nations, baptizing them in the name of the Father and of the Son and of the Holy Spirit,

(Matthew 28:19)

[192]For I received from the Lord what I also delivered to you, that the Lord Jesus on the night when he was betrayed took bread, and when he had given thanks, he broke it, and said, "This is my body which is for you. Do this in remembrance of me." In the same way also he took the cup, after supper, saying, "This cup is the new covenant in my blood. Do this, as often as you drink it, in remembrance of me." For as often as you eat this bread and drink the cup, you proclaim the Lord's death until he comes.

(1 Corinthians 11:23-26)

Q 94 What is baptism?

A Baptism is a sacrament, wherein the washing with water in the name of the Father, and of the Son, and of the Holy Ghost,[193] **doth signify and seal our ingrafting into Christ, and partaking of the benefits of the covenant of grace, and our engagement to be the Lord's** [194]

[193] Go therefore and make disciples of all nations, baptizing them in the name of the Father and of the Son and of the Holy Spirit,

(Matthew 28:19)

[194] And Peter said to them, "Repent and be baptized every one of you in the name of Jesus Christ for the forgiveness of your sins, and you will receive the gift of the Holy Spirit. For the promise is for you and for your children and for all who are far off, everyone whom the Lord our God calls to himself." And with many other words he bore witness and continued to exhort them, saying, "Save yourselves from this crooked generation." So those who received his word were baptized, and there were added that day about three thousand souls. And they devoted themselves to the apostles' teaching and the fellowship, to the breaking of bread and the prayers.

(Acts 2:38-42)

And now why do you wait? Rise and be baptized and wash away your sins, calling on his name.'

(Acts 22:16)

Do you not know that all of us who have been baptized into Christ Jesus were baptized into his death? We were buried therefore with him by baptism into death, in order that, just as Christ was raised from the dead by the glory of the Father, we too might walk in newness of life.

(Romans 6:3-4)

for in Christ Jesus you are all sons of God, through faith. For as many of you as were baptized into Christ have put on Christ.

(Galatians 3:26-27)

Baptism, which corresponds to this, now saves you, not as a removal of dirt from the body but as an appeal to God for a good conscience, through the resurrection of Jesus Christ,

(1 Peter 3:21)

Q 95 To whom is Baptism to be administered?

A Baptism is not to be administered to any that are out of the visible church, till they profess their faith in Christ, and obedience to him;[195] **but the infants of such as are members of the visible church are to be baptized** [196]

[195] So those who received his word were baptized, and there were added that day about three thousand souls.

(Acts 2:41)

But when they believed Philip as he preached good news about the kingdom of God and the name of Jesus Christ, they were baptized, both men and women.

(Acts 8:12)

And as they were going along the road they came to some water, and the eunuch said, "See, here is water! What prevents me from being baptized?"

(Acts 8:36)

And he commanded the chariot to stop, and they both went down into the water, Philip and the eunuch, and he baptized him.

(Acts 8:38)

Crispus, the ruler of the synagogue, believed in the Lord, together with his entire household. And many of the Corinthians hearing Paul believed and were baptized.

(Acts 18:8)

(196) And I will establish my covenant between me and you and your offspring after you throughout their generations for an everlasting covenant, to be God to you and to your offspring after you.

(Genesis 17:7)

And God said to Abraham, "As for you, you shall keep my covenant, you and your offspring after you throughout their generations. This is my covenant, which you shall keep, between me and you and your offspring after you: Every male among you shall be circumcised. You shall be circumcised in the flesh of your foreskins, and it shall be a sign of the covenant between me and you.

(Genesis 17:9-11)

And Peter said to them, "Repent and be baptized every one of you in the name of Jesus Christ for the forgiveness of your sins, and you will receive the gift of the Holy Spirit. For the promise is for you and for your children and for all who are far off, everyone whom the Lord our God calls to himself."

(Acts 2:38-39)

And they spoke the word of the Lord to him and to all who were in his house. And he took them the same hour of the night and washed their wounds; and he was baptized at once, he and all his family.

(Acts 16:32-33)

In him also you were circumcised with a circumcision made without hands, by putting off the body of the flesh, by the circumcision of Christ, having been buried with him in baptism, in which you were also raised with him through faith in the powerful working of God, who raised him from the dead.

(Colossians 2:11-12)

Q 96 What is the Lord's Supper?

A The Lord's Supper is a sacrament, wherein, by giving and receiving bread and wine, according to Christ's appointment, his death is showed forth;(197) and the worthy receivers are, not after a corporal and carnal manner, but by faith, made partakers of his body and blood, with all his benefits, to their spiritual nourishment, and growth in grace (198)

(197) And he took bread, and when he had given thanks, he broke it and gave it to them, saying, "This is my body, which is given for you. Do this in remembrance of me." And likewise the cup after they had eaten, saying, "This cup that is poured out for you is the new covenant in my blood.

(Luke 22:19-20)

For I received from the Lord what I also delivered to you, that the Lord Jesus on the night when he was betrayed took bread, and when he had given thanks, he broke it, and said, "This is my body which is for you. Do this in remembrance of me." In the same way also he took the cup, after supper, saying, "This cup is the new covenant in my blood. Do this, as often as you drink it, in remembrance of me." For as often as you eat this bread and drink the cup, you proclaim the Lord's death until he comes.

(1 Corinthians 11:23-26)

(198) The cup of blessing that we bless, is it not a participation in the blood of Christ? The bread that we break, is it not a participation in the body of Christ?

(1 Corinthians 10:16)

Q 97 What is required for the worthy receiving of the Lord's Supper?

A It is required of them that would worthily partake of the Lord's Supper, that they examine themselves of their knowledge to discern the Lord's body, of their faith to feed upon him, of their repentance, love, and new obedience; lest, coming unworthily, they eat and drink judgment to themselves (199)

(199) Whoever, therefore, eats the bread or drinks the cup of the Lord in an unworthy manner will be guilty concerning the body and blood of the Lord. Let a person examine himself, then, and so eat of the bread and drink of the cup. For anyone who eats and drinks without discerning the body eats and drinks judgment on himself. That is why many of you are weak and ill, and some have died. But if we judged ourselves truly, we would not be judged.

(1 Corinthians 11:27-31)

Q 98 What is prayer?

A Prayer is an offering up of our desires unto God,[200] **for things agreeable to his will,**[201] **in the name of Christ,**[202] **with confession of our sins,**[203] **and thankful acknowledgment of his mercies**[204]

[200] O LORD, you hear the desire of the afflicted; you will strengthen their heart; you will incline your ear

(Psalms 10:17)

Trust in him at all times, O people; pour out your heart before him; God is a refuge for us. Selah

(Psalms 62:8)

"Ask, and it will be given to you; seek, and you will find; knock, and it will be opened to you. For everyone who asks receives, and the one who seeks finds, and to the one who knocks it will be opened.

(Matthew 7:7-8)

[201] And this is the confidence that we have toward him, that if we ask anything according to his will he hears us.

(1 John 5:14)

[202] In that day you will ask nothing of me. Truly, truly, I say to you, whatever you ask of the Father in my name, he will give it to you. Until now you have asked nothing in my name. Ask, and you will receive, that your joy may be full.

(John 16:23-24)

(203) I acknowledged my sin to you, and I did not cover my iniquity; I said, "I will confess my transgressions to the LORD," and you forgave the iniquity of my sin. Selah Therefore let everyone who is godly offer prayer to you at a time when you may be found; surely in the rush of great waters, they shall not reach him.

(Psalms 32:5-6)

I prayed to the LORD my God and made confession, saying, "O Lord, the great and awesome God, who keeps covenant and steadfast love with those who love him and keep his commandments, we have sinned and done wrong and acted wickedly and rebelled, turning aside from your commandments and rules. We have not listened to your servants the prophets, who spoke in your name to our kings, our princes, and our fathers, and to all the people of the land. To you, O Lord, belongs righteousness, but to us open shame, as at this day, to the men of Judah, to the inhabitants of Jerusalem, and to all Israel, those who are near and those who are far away, in all the lands to which you have driven them, because of the treachery that they have committed against you. To us, O LORD, belongs open shame, to our kings, to our princes, and to our fathers, because we have sinned against you. To the Lord our God belong mercy and forgiveness, for we have rebelled against him and have not obeyed the voice of the LORD our God by walking in his laws, which he set before us by his servants the prophets. All Israel has transgressed your law and turned aside, refusing to obey your voice. And the curse and oath that are written in the Law of Moses the servant of God have been poured out upon us, because we have sinned against him. He has confirmed his words, which he spoke against us and against our rulers who ruled us, by bringing upon us a great calamity. For under the whole heaven there has not been done anything like what has been done against Jerusalem. As it is written in the Law of Moses, all this calamity has come upon us; yet we have not entreated the favor of the LORD our God, turning from our iniquities and gaining insight by your truth. Therefore the LORD has kept ready the calamity and has brought it upon us, for the LORD our God is righteous in all the works that he has done, and we have not obeyed his voice. And now, O Lord our God, who brought your people out of the land of Egypt with a mighty hand, and have made a name for yourself, as at this day, we have sinned, we have done wickedly. "O Lord, according to all your righteous acts, let your anger and your wrath turn away from your city Jerusalem, your holy hill, because for our sins, and for the iniquities of our fathers, Jerusalem and your people have become a byword among all who are around us. Now therefore, O our God, listen to the prayer of your servant and to his pleas for mercy, and for your own sake, O Lord, make your face to shine upon your sanctuary, which is desolate. O my God, incline your ear and hear. Open your eyes and see our desolations, and the city that is called by your name. For we do not present our pleas before you because of our righteousness, but because of your great mercy. O Lord, hear; O Lord, forgive. O Lord, pay attention and act. Delay not, for your own sake, O my God, because your city and your people are called by your name."

(Daniel 9:4-19)

The true light, which enlightens everyone, was coming into the world.

(John 1:9)

(204) Of David. Bless the LORD, O my soul, and all that is within me, bless his holy name! Bless the LORD, O my soul, and forget not all his benefits, who forgives all your iniquity, who heals all your diseases, who redeems your life from the pit, who crowns you with steadfast love and mercy, who satisfies you with good so that your youth is renewed like the eagle's.

(Psalms 103:1-5)

Give thanks to the LORD, for he is good, for his steadfast love endures forever. Give thanks to the God of gods, for his steadfast love endures forever. Give thanks to the Lord of lords, for his steadfast love endures forever; to him who alone does great wonders, for his steadfast love endures forever; to him who by understanding made the heavens, for his steadfast love endures forever; to him who spread out the earth above the waters, for his steadfast love endures forever; to him who made the great lights, for his steadfast love endures forever; the sun to rule over the day, for his steadfast love endures forever; the moon and stars to rule over the night, for his steadfast love endures forever; to him who struck down the firstborn of Egypt, for his steadfast love endures forever; and brought Israel out from among them, for his steadfast love endures forever; with a strong hand and an outstretched arm, for his steadfast love endures forever; to him who divided the Red Sea in two, for his steadfast love endures forever; and made Israel pass through the midst of it, for his steadfast love endures forever; but overthrew Pharaoh and his host in the Red Sea, for his steadfast love endures forever; to him who led his people through the wilderness, for his steadfast love endures forever; to him who struck down great kings, for his steadfast love endures forever; and killed mighty kings, for his steadfast love endures forever; Sihon, king of the Amorites, for his steadfast love endures forever; and Og, king of Bashan, for his steadfast love endures forever; and gave their land as a heritage, for his steadfast love endures forever; a heritage to Israel his servant, for his steadfast love endures forever. It is he who remembered us in our low estate, for his steadfast love endures forever; and rescued us from our foes, for his steadfast love endures forever; he who gives food to all flesh, for his steadfast love endures forever. Give thanks to the God of heaven, for his steadfast love endures forever.

(Psalms 136:1-26)

do not be anxious about anything, but in everything by prayer and supplication with thanksgiving let your requests be made known to God.

(Philippians 4:6)

Q 99 What rule hath God given for our direction in prayer?

A The whole Word of God is of use to direct us in prayer;[205] but the special rule of direction is that form of prayer which Christ taught his disciples, commonly called the Lord's Prayer [206]

[205] And this is the confidence that we have toward him, that if we ask anything according to his will he hears us.

(1 John 5:14)

[206] Pray then like this: "Our Father in heaven, hallowed be your name. Your kingdom come, your will be done, on earth as it is in heaven. Give us this day our daily bread, and forgive us our debts, as we also have forgiven our debtors. And lead us not into temptation, but deliver us from evil.

(Matthew 6:9-13)

Q 100 What doth the preface of the Lord's Prayer teach us?

A The preface of the Lord's Prayer, which is, Our Father which art in heaven, teacheth us to draw near to God with all holy reverence[207] and confidence,[208] as children to a father,[209] able and ready to help us;[210] and that we should pray with and for others [211]

[207] Oh come, let us worship and bow down; let us kneel before the LORD, our Maker!

(Psalms 95:6)

[208] in whom we have boldness and access with confidence through our faith in him.

(Ephesians 3:12)

[209] Or which one of you, if his son asks him for bread, will give him a stone? Or if he asks for a fish, will give him a serpent? If you then, who are evil, know how to give good gifts to your children, how much more will your Father who is in heaven give good things to those who ask him!

(Matthew 7:9-11)

What father among you, if his son asks for a fish, will instead of a fish give him a serpent; or if he asks for an egg, will give him a scorpion? If you then, who are evil, know how to give good gifts to your children, how much more will the heavenly Father give the Holy Spirit to those who ask him!"

(Luke 11:11-13)

For you did not receive the spirit of slavery to fall back into fear, but you have received the Spirit of adoption as sons, by whom we cry, "Abba! Father!"

(Romans 8:15)

(210) Now to him who is able to do far more abundantly than all that we ask or think, according to the power at work within us,

(Ephesians 3:20)

(211) praying at all times in the Spirit, with all prayer and supplication. To that end keep alert with all perseverance, making supplication for all the saints,

(Ephesians 6:18)

Q 101 What do we pray for in the first petition?

A In the first petition, which is, Hallowed be thy name, we pray that God would enable us, and others, to glorify him in all that whereby he maketh himself known;(212) and that he would dispose all things to his own glory (213)

(212) To the choirmaster: with stringed instruments. A Psalm. A Song. May God be gracious to us and bless us and make his face to shine upon us, Selah that your way may be known on earth, your saving power among all nations. Let the peoples praise you, O God; let all the peoples praise you!

(Psalms 67:1-3)

Let them praise your great and awesome name! Holy is he!

(Psalms 99:3)

Know that the LORD, he is God! It is he who made us, and we are his; we are his people, and the sheep of his pasture. Enter his gates with thanksgiving, and his courts with praise! Give thanks to him; bless his name!

(Psalms 100:3-4)

(213) Oh, the depth of the riches and wisdom and knowledge of God! How unsearchable are his judgments and how inscrutable his ways!

(Romans 11:33)

"Worthy are you, our Lord and God, to receive glory and honor and power, for you created all things, and by your will they existed and were created."

(Revelation 4:11)

Q 102 What do we pray for in the second petition?

A In the second petition, which is, Thy kingdom come, we pray that Satan's kingdom may be destroyed;(214) and that the kingdom of grace may be advanced,(215) ourselves and others brought into it, and kept in it;(216) and that the kingdom of glory may be hastened (217)

(214) Knowing their thoughts, he said to them, "Every kingdom divided against itself is laid waste, and no city or house divided against itself will stand. And if Satan casts out Satan, he is divided against himself. How then will his kingdom stand? And if I cast out demons by Beelzebul, by whom do your sons cast them out? Therefore they will be your judges. But if it is by the Spirit of God that I cast out demons, then the kingdom of God has come upon you.

(Matthew 12:25-28)

The God of peace will soon crush Satan under your feet. The grace of our Lord Jesus Christ be with you.

(Romans 16:20)

Whoever makes a practice of sinning is of the devil, for the devil has been sinning from the beginning. The reason the Son of God appeared was to destroy the works of the devil.

(1 John 3:8)

(215) May he have dominion from sea to sea, and from the River to the ends of the earth! May desert tribes bow down before him, and his enemies lick the dust! May the kings of Tarshish and of the coastlands render him tribute; may the kings of Sheba and Seba bring gifts! May all kings fall down before him, all nations serve him!

(Psalms 72:8-11)

And this gospel of the kingdom will be proclaimed throughout the whole world as a testimony to all nations, and then the end will come.

(Matthew 24:14)

And this gospel of the kingdom will be proclaimed throughout the whole world as a testimony to all nations, and then the end will come. "So when you see the abomination of desolation spoken of by the prophet Daniel, standing in the holy place (let the reader understand),

(Matthew 24:14-15)

(216) Oh that my ways may be steadfast in keeping your statutes!

(Psalms 119:5)

but I have prayed for you that your faith may not fail. And when you have turned again, strengthen your brothers."

(Luke 22:32)

Finally, brothers, pray for us, that the word of the Lord may speed ahead and be honored, as happened among you,

(2 Thessalonians 3:1)

(217) He who testifies to these things says, "Surely I am coming soon." Amen. Come, Lord Jesus!

(Revelation 22:20)

Q 103 What do we pray for in the third petition?

A In the third petition, which is, Thy will be done in earth, as it is in heaven, we pray that God, by his grace, would make us able and willing to know, obey, and submit to his will in all things,(218) as the angels do in heaven (219)

(218) Let the words of my mouth and the meditation of my heart be acceptable in your sight, O LORD, my rock and my redeemer.

(Psalms 19:14)

Psalms 119:1-176

(1) Blessed are those whose way is blameless, who walk in the law of the LORD!

(2) Blessed are those who keep his testimonies, who seek him with their whole heart,

(3) who also do no wrong, but walk in his ways!

(4) You have commanded your precepts to be kept diligently.

(5) Oh that my ways may be steadfast in keeping your statutes!

(6) Then I shall not be put to shame, having my eyes fixed on all your commandments.

(7) I will praise you with an upright heart, when I learn your righteous rules.

(8) I will keep your statutes; do not utterly forsake me!

(9) How can a young man keep his way pure? By guarding it according to your word.

(10) With my whole heart I seek you; let me not wander from your commandments!

(11) I have stored up your word in my heart, that I might not sin against you.

(12) Blessed are you, O LORD; teach me your statutes!

(13) With my lips I declare all the rules of your mouth.

(14) In the way of your testimonies I delight as much as in all riches.

(15) I will meditate on your precepts and fix my eyes on your ways.

(16) I will delight in your statutes; I will not forget your word.

(17) Deal bountifully with your servant, that I may live and keep your word.

(18) Open my eyes, that I may behold wondrous things out of your law.

(19) I am a sojourner on the earth; hide not your commandments from me!

(20) My soul is consumed with longing for your rules at all times.

(21) You rebuke the insolent, accursed ones, who wander from your commandments.

(22) Take away from me scorn and contempt, for I have kept your testimonies.

(23) Even though princes sit plotting against me, your servant will meditate on your statutes.

(24) Your testimonies are my delight; they are my counselors.

(25) My soul clings to the dust; give me life according to your word!

(26) When I told of my ways, you answered me; teach me your statutes!

(27) Make me understand the way of your precepts, and I will meditate on your wondrous works.

(28) My soul melts away for sorrow; strengthen me according to your word!

(29) Put false ways far from me and graciously teach me your law!

(30) I have chosen the way of faithfulness; I set your rules before me.

(31) I cling to your testimonies, O LORD; let me not be put to shame!

(32) I will run in the way of your commandments when you enlarge my heart!

(33) Teach me, O LORD, the way of your statutes; and I will keep it to the end.

(34) Give me understanding, that I may keep your law and observe it with my whole heart.

(35) Lead me in the path of your commandments, for I delight in it.

(36) Incline my heart to your testimonies, and not to selfish gain!

(37) Turn my eyes from looking at worthless things; and give me life in your ways.

(38) Confirm to your servant your promise, that you may be feared.

(39) Turn away the reproach that I dread, for your rules are good.

(40) Behold, I long for your precepts; in your righteousness give me life!

(41) Let your steadfast love come to me, O LORD, your salvation according to your promise;

(42) then shall I have an answer for him who taunts me, for I trust in your word.

(43) And take not the word of truth utterly out of my mouth, for my hope is in your rules.

(44) I will keep your law continually, forever and ever,

(45) and I shall walk in a wide place, for I have sought your precepts.

(46) I will also speak of your testimonies before kings and shall not be put to shame,

(47) for I find my delight in your commandments, which I love.

(48) I will lift up my hands toward your commandments, which I love, and I will meditate on your statutes.

(49) Remember your word to your servant, in which you have made me hope.

(50) This is my comfort in my affliction, that your promise gives me life.

(51) The insolent utterly deride me, but I do not turn away from your law.

(52) When I think of your rules from of old, I take comfort, O LORD.

(53) Hot indignation seizes me because of the wicked, who forsake your law.

(54) Your statutes have been my songs in the house of my sojourning.

(55) I remember your name in the night, O LORD, and keep your law.

(56) This blessing has fallen to me, that I have kept your precepts.

(57) The LORD is my portion; I promise to keep your words.

(58) I entreat your favor with all my heart; be gracious to me according to your promise.

(59) When I think on my ways, I turn my feet to your testimonies;

(60) I hasten and do not delay to keep your commandments.

(61) Though the cords of the wicked ensnare me, I do not forget your law.

(62) At midnight I rise to praise you, because of your righteous rules.

(63) I am a companion of all who fear you, of those who keep your precepts.

(64) The earth, O LORD, is full of your steadfast love; teach me your statutes!

(65) You have dealt well with your servant, O LORD, according to your word.

(66) Teach me good judgment and knowledge, for I believe in your commandments.

(67) Before I was afflicted I went astray, but now I keep your word.

(68) You are good and do good; teach me your statutes.

(69) The insolent smear me with lies, but with my whole heart I keep your precepts;

(70) their heart is unfeeling like fat, but I delight in your law.

(71) It is good for me that I was afflicted, that I might learn your statutes.

(72) The law of your mouth is better to me than thousands of gold and silver pieces.

(73) Your hands have made and fashioned me; give me understanding that I may learn your commandments.

(74) Those who fear you shall see me and rejoice, because I have hoped in your word.

(75) I know, O LORD, that your rules are righteous, and that in faithfulness you have afflicted me.

(76) Let your steadfast love comfort me according to your promise to your servant.

(77) Let your mercy come to me, that I may live; for your law is my delight.

(78) Let the insolent be put to shame, because they have wronged me with falsehood; as for me, I will meditate on your precepts.

(79) Let those who fear you turn to me, that they may know your testimonies.

(80) May my heart be blameless in your statutes, that I may not be put to shame!

(81) My soul longs for your salvation; I hope in your word.

(82) My eyes long for your promise; I ask, "When will you comfort me?"

(83) For I have become like a wineskin in the smoke, yet I have not forgotten your statutes.

(84) How long must your servant endure? When will you judge those who persecute me?

(85) The insolent have dug pitfalls for me; they do not live according to your law.

(86) All your commandments are sure; they persecute me with falsehood; help me!

(87) They have almost made an end of me on earth, but I have not forsaken your precepts.

(88) In your steadfast love give me life, that I may keep the testimonies of your mouth.

(89) Forever, O LORD, your word is firmly fixed in the heavens.

(90) Your faithfulness endures to all generations; you have established the earth, and it stands fast.

(91) By your appointment they stand this day, for all things are your servants.

(92) If your law had not been my delight, I would have perished in my affliction.

(93) I will never forget your precepts, for by them you have given me life.

(94) I am yours; save me, for I have sought your precepts.

(95) The wicked lie in wait to destroy me, but I consider your testimonies.

(96) I have seen a limit to all perfection, but your commandment is exceedingly broad.

(97) Oh how I love your law! It is my meditation all the day.

(98) Your commandment makes me wiser than my enemies, for it is ever with me.

(99) I have more understanding than all my teachers, for your testimonies are my meditation.

(100) I understand more than the aged, for I keep your precepts.

(101) I hold back my feet from every evil way, in order to keep your word.

(102) I do not turn aside from your rules, for you have taught me.

(103) How sweet are your words to my taste, sweeter than honey to my mouth!

(104) Through your precepts I get understanding; therefore I hate every false way.

(105) Your word is a lamp to my feet and a light to my path.

(106) I have sworn an oath and confirmed it, to keep your righteous rules.

(107) I am severely afflicted; give me life, O LORD, according to your word!

(108) Accept my freewill offerings of praise, O LORD, and teach me your rules.

(109) I hold my life in my hand continually, but I do not forget your law.

(110) The wicked have laid a snare for me, but I do not stray from your precepts.

(111) Your testimonies are my heritage forever, for they are the joy of my heart.

(112) I incline my heart to perform your statutes forever, to the end.

(113) I hate the double-minded, but I love your law.

(114) You are my hiding place and my shield; I hope in your word.

(115) Depart from me, you evildoers, that I may keep the commandments of my God.

(116) Uphold me according to your promise, that I may live, and let me not be put to shame in my hope!

(117) Hold me up, that I may be safe and have regard for your statutes continually!

(118) You spurn all who go astray from your statutes, for their cunning is in vain.

(119) All the wicked of the earth you discard like dross, therefore I love your testimonies.

(120) My flesh trembles for fear of you, and I am afraid of your judgments.

(121) I have done what is just and right; do not leave me to my oppressors.

(122) Give your servant a pledge of good; let not the insolent oppress me.

(123) My eyes long for your salvation and for the fulfillment of your righteous promise.

(124) Deal with your servant according to your steadfast love, and teach me your statutes.

(125) I am your servant; give me understanding, that I may know your testimonies!

(126) It is time for the LORD to act, for your law has been broken.

(127) Therefore I love your commandments above gold, above fine gold.

(128) Therefore I consider all your precepts to be right; I hate every false way.

(129) Your testimonies are wonderful; therefore my soul keeps them.

(130) The unfolding of your words gives light; it imparts understanding to the simple.

(131) I open my mouth and pant, because I long for your commandments.

(132) Turn to me and be gracious to me, as is your way with those who love your name.

(133) Keep steady my steps according to your promise, and let no iniquity get dominion over me.

(134) Redeem me from man's oppression, that I may keep your precepts.

(135) Make your face shine upon your servant, and teach me your statutes.

(136) My eyes shed streams of tears, because people do not keep your law.

(137) Righteous are you, O LORD, and right are your rules.

(138) You have appointed your testimonies in righteousness and in all faithfulness.

(139) My zeal consumes me, because my foes forget your words.

(140) Your promise is well tried, and your servant loves it.

(141) I am small and despised, yet I do not forget your precepts.

(142) Your righteousness is righteous forever, and your law is true.

(143) Trouble and anguish have found me out, but your commandments are my delight.

(144) Your testimonies are righteous forever; give me understanding that I may live.

(145) With my whole heart I cry; answer me, O LORD! I will keep your statutes.

(146) I call to you; save me, that I may observe your testimonies.

(147) I rise before dawn and cry for help; I hope in your words.

(148) My eyes are awake before the watches of the night, that I may meditate on your promise.

(149) Hear my voice according to your steadfast love; O LORD, according to your justice give me life.

(150) They draw near who persecute me with evil purpose; they are far from your law.

(151) But you are near, O LORD, and all your commandments are true.

(152) Long have I known from your testimonies that you have founded them forever.

(153) Look on my affliction and deliver me, for I do not forget your law.

(154) Plead my cause and redeem me; give me life according to your promise!

(155) Salvation is far from the wicked, for they do not seek your statutes.

(156) Great is your mercy, O LORD; give me life according to your rules.

(157) Many are my persecutors and my adversaries, but I do not swerve from your testimonies.

(158) I look at the faithless with disgust, because they do not keep your commands.

(159) Consider how I love your precepts! Give me life according to your steadfast love.

(160) The sum of your word is truth, and every one of your righteous rules endures forever.

(161) Princes persecute me without cause, but my heart stands in awe of your words.

(162) I rejoice at your word like one who finds great spoil.

(163) I hate and abhor falsehood, but I love your law.

(164) Seven times a day I praise you for your righteous rules.

(165) Great peace have those who love your law; nothing can make them stumble.

(166) I hope for your salvation, O LORD, and I do your commandments.

(167) My soul keeps your testimonies; I love them exceedingly.

(168) I keep your precepts and testimonies, for all my ways are before you.

(169) Let my cry come before you, O LORD; give me understanding according to your word!

(170) Let my plea come before you; deliver me according to your word.

(171) My lips will pour forth praise, for you teach me your statutes.

(172) My tongue will sing of your word, for all your commandments are right.

(173) Let your hand be ready to help me, for I have chosen your precepts.

(174) I long for your salvation, O LORD, and your law is my delight.

(175) Let my soul live and praise you, and let your rules help me.

(176) I have gone astray like a lost sheep; seek your servant, for I do not forget your commandments.

Now may the God of peace himself sanctify you completely, and may your whole spirit and soul and body be kept blameless at the coming of our Lord Jesus Christ.

(1 Thessalonians 5:23)

Now may the God of peace who brought again from the dead our Lord Jesus, the great shepherd of the sheep, by the blood of the eternal covenant, equip you with everything good that you may do his will, working in us that which is pleasing in his sight, through Jesus Christ, to whom be glory forever and ever. Amen.

(Hebrews 13:20-21)

(219) Bless the LORD, O you his angels, you mighty ones who do his word, obeying the voice of his word! Bless the LORD, all his hosts, his ministers, who do his will!

(Psalms 103:20-21)

Are they not all ministering spirits sent out to serve for the sake of those who are to inherit salvation?

(Hebrews 1:14)

Q 104 What do we pray for in the fourth petition?

A In the fourth petition, which is,' Give us this day our daily bread,' we pray that of God's free gift we may receive a competent portion of the good things of this life, and enjoy his blessing with them.[220]

[220] Remove far from me falsehood and lying; give me neither poverty nor riches; feed me with the food that is needful for me, lest I be full and deny you and say, "Who is the LORD?" or lest I be poor and steal and profane the name of my God.

(Proverbs 30:8-9)

Therefore do not be anxious, saying, 'What shall we eat?' or 'What shall we drink?' or 'What shall we wear?' For the Gentiles seek after all these things, and your heavenly Father knows that you need them all. But seek first the kingdom of God and his righteousness, and all these things will be added to you. "Therefore do not be anxious about tomorrow, for tomorrow will be anxious for itself. Sufficient for the day is its own trouble.

(Matthew 6:31-34)

Not that I am speaking of being in need, for I have learned in whatever situation I am to be content.

(Philippians 4:11)

And my God will supply every need of yours according to his riches in glory in Christ Jesus.

(Philippians 4:19)

Now there is great gain in godliness with contentment, for we brought nothing into the world, and we cannot take anything out of the world. But if we have food and clothing, with these we will be content.

(1 Timothy 6:6-8)

Q 105 What do we pray for in the fifth petition?

A In the fifth petition, which is, And forgive us our debts, as we forgive our debtors, we pray that God, for Christ's sake, would freely pardon all our sins;(221) which we are the rather encouraged to ask, because by his grace we are enabled from the heart to forgive others (222)

(221) To the choirmaster. A Psalm of David, when Nathan the prophet went to him, after he had gone in to Bathsheba. Have mercy on me, O God, according to your steadfast love; according to your abundant mercy blot out my transgressions. Wash me thoroughly from my iniquity, and cleanse me from my sin!

(Psalms 51:1-2)

Purge me with hyssop, and I shall be clean; wash me, and I shall be whiter than snow.

(Psalms 51:7)

Hide your face from my sins, and blot out all my iniquities.

(Psalms 51:9)

Now therefore, O our God, listen to the prayer of your servant and to his pleas for mercy, and for your own sake, O Lord, make your face to shine upon your sanctuary, which is desolate. O my God, incline your ear and hear. Open your eyes and see our desolations, and the city that is called by your name. For we do not present our pleas before you because of our righteousness, but because of your great mercy. O Lord, hear; O Lord, forgive. O Lord, pay attention and act. Delay not, for your own sake, O my God, because your city and your people are called by your name."

(Daniel 9:17-19)

But if we walk in the light, as he is in the light, we have fellowship with one another, and the blood of Jesus his Son cleanses us from all sin.

(1 John 1:7)

(222) Then Peter came up and said to him, "Lord, how often will my brother sin against me, and I forgive him? As many as seven times?" Jesus said to him, "I do not say to you seven times, but seventy times seven. "Therefore the kingdom of heaven may be compared to a king who wished to settle accounts with his servants. When he began to settle, one was brought to him who owed him ten thousand talents. And since he could not pay, his master ordered him to be sold, with his wife and children and all that he had, and payment to be made. So the servant fell on his knees, imploring him, 'Have patience with me, and I will pay you everything.' And out of pity for him, the master of that servant released him and forgave him the debt. But when that same servant went out, he found one of his fellow servants who owed him a hundred denarii, and seizing him, he began to choke him, saying, 'Pay what you owe.' So his fellow servant fell down and pleaded with him, 'Have patience with me, and I will pay you.' He refused and went and put him in prison until he should pay the debt. When his fellow servants saw what had taken place, they were greatly distressed, and they went and reported to their master all that had taken place. Then his master summoned him and said to him, 'You wicked servant! I forgave you all that debt because you pleaded with me. And should not you have had mercy on your fellow servant, as I had mercy on you?' And in anger his master delivered him to the jailers, until he should pay all his debt. So also my heavenly Father will do to every one of you, if you do not forgive your brother from your heart."

(Matthew 18:21-35)

Be kind to one another, tenderhearted, forgiving one another, as God in Christ forgave you.

(Ephesians 4:32)

bearing with one another and, if one has a complaint against another, forgiving each other; as the Lord has forgiven you, so you also must forgive.

(Colossians 3:13)

Q 106 What do we pray for in the sixth petition?

A In the sixth petition, which is, And lead us not into temptation, but deliver us from evil, we pray that God would either keep us from being tempted to sin,[223] or support and deliver us when we are tempted [224]

[223] Keep back your servant also from presumptuous sins; let them not have dominion over me! Then I shall be blameless, and innocent of great transgression.

(Psalms 19:13)

Watch and pray that you may not enter into temptation. The spirit indeed is willing, but the flesh is weak."

(Matthew 26:41)

I do not ask that you take them out of the world, but that you keep them from the evil one.

(John 17:15)

[224] "Simon, Simon, behold, Satan demanded to have you, that he might sift you like wheat, but I have prayed for you that your faith may not fail. And when you have turned again, strengthen your brothers."

(Luke 22:31-32)

No temptation has overtaken you that is not common to man. God is faithful, and he will not let you be tempted beyond your ability, but with the temptation he will also provide the way of escape, that you may be able to endure it.

(1 Corinthians 10:13)

So to keep me from becoming conceited because of the surpassing greatness of the revelations, a thorn was given me in the flesh, a messenger of Satan to harass me, to keep me from becoming conceited. Three times I pleaded with the Lord about this, that it should leave me. But he said to me, "My grace is sufficient for you, for my power is made perfect in weakness." Therefore I will boast all the more gladly of my weaknesses, so that the power of Christ may rest upon me.

(2 Corinthians 12:7-9)

For because he himself has suffered when tempted, he is able to help those who are being tempted.

(Hebrews 2:18)

Q 107 What doth the conclusion of the Lord's Prayer teach us?

A **The conclusion of the Lord's Prayer, which is, For thine is the kingdom, and the power, and the glory, forever Amen, teacheth us to take our encouragement in prayer from God only,(225) and in our prayers to praise him, ascribing kingdom, power, and glory to him;(226) and, in testimony of our desire, and assurance to be heard, we say, Amen (227)**

(225) I prayed to the LORD my God and made confession, saying, "O Lord, the great and awesome God, who keeps covenant and steadfast love with those who love him and keep his commandments,

(Daniel 9:4)

To you, O Lord, belongs righteousness, but to us open shame, as at this day, to the men of Judah, to the inhabitants of Jerusalem, and to all Israel, those who are near and those who are far away, in all the lands to which you have driven them, because of the treachery that they have committed against you. To us, O LORD, belongs open shame, to our kings, to our princes, and to our fathers, because we have sinned against you. To the Lord our God belong mercy and forgiveness, for we have rebelled against him

(Daniel 9:7-9)

"O Lord, according to all your righteous acts, let your anger and your wrath turn away from your city Jerusalem, your holy hill, because for our sins, and for the iniquities of our fathers, Jerusalem and your people have become a byword among all who are around us. Now therefore, O our God, listen to the prayer of your servant and to his pleas for mercy, and for your own sake, O Lord, make your face to shine upon your sanctuary, which is desolate. O my God, incline your ear and hear. Open your eyes and see our desolations, and the city that is called by your name. For we do not present our pleas before you because of our righteousness, but because of your great mercy. O Lord, hear; O Lord, forgive. O Lord, pay attention and act. Delay not, for your own sake, O my God, because your city and your people are called by your name."

(Daniel 9:16-19)

And he told them a parable to the effect that they ought always to pray and not lose heart.

(Luke 18:1)

And will not God give justice to his elect, who cry to him day and night? Will he delay long over them? I tell you, he will give justice to them speedily. Nevertheless, when the Son of Man comes, will he find faith on earth?"

(Luke 18:7-8)

(226) Therefore David blessed the LORD in the presence of all the assembly. And David said: "Blessed are you, O LORD, the God of Israel our father, forever and ever. Yours, O LORD, is the greatness and the power and the glory and the victory and the majesty, for all that is in the heavens and in the earth is yours. Yours is the kingdom, O LORD, and you are exalted as head above all. Both riches and honor come from you, and you rule over all. In your hand are power and might, and in your hand it is to make great and to give strength to all. And now we thank you, our God, and praise your glorious name.

(1 Chronicles 29:10-13)

To the King of ages, immortal, invisible, the only God, be honor and glory forever and ever. Amen.

(1 Timothy 1:17)

Then I looked, and I heard around the throne and the living creatures and the elders the voice of many angels, numbering myriads of myriads and thousands of thousands, saying with a loud voice, "Worthy is the Lamb who was slain, to receive power and wealth and wisdom and might and honor and glory and blessing!" And I heard every creature in heaven and on earth and under the earth and in the sea, and all that is in them, saying, "To him who sits on the throne and to the Lamb be blessing and honor and glory and might forever and ever!"

(Revelation 5:11-13)

[227] Otherwise, if you give thanks with your spirit, how can anyone in the position of an outsider say "Amen" to your thanksgiving when he does not know what you are saying?

(1 Corinthians 14:16)

He who testifies to these things says, "Surely I am coming soon." Amen. Come, Lord Jesus!

(Revelation 22:20)

Index

---

exaltation, 70, 84

faith, 16, 17, 28, 38, 87, 88, 90, 95, 96, 101, 102, 158, 169, 173, 175, 176, 181, 183, 184, 191, 192, 193, 195, 196, 202, 207, 228, 231

fall, 11, 48, 50, 54, 56, 130, 169, 203, 206

Father, 20, 24, 30, 32, 33, 56, 64, 65, 70, 71, 73, 78, 79, 84, 85, 90, 91, 97, 99, 105, 112, 127, 166, 180, 187, 189, 190, 197, 201, 202, 203, 222, 226

fathers, 27, 62, 70, 119, 121, 136, 139, 178, 198, 230

fell, 45, 47, 48, 52, 56, 177, 226

flesh, 11, 13, 20, 33, 53, 54, 57, 65, 67, 77, 78, 91, 99, 122, 151, 175, 193, 200, 228, 229

forbidden, 47, 116, 121, 130, 139, 148, 152, 155, 158, 163, 168

forbidding, 44

foreordained, 35

forever, 10, 15, 22, 23, 24, 29, 32, 33, 35, 56, 60, 64, 66, 71, 107, 114, 117, 127, 131, 133, 143, 199, 221, 230, 231, 232

forgive, 62, 179, 199, 201, 225, 226, 227, 230

freedom, 45, 59

fruit, 45, 47, 87, 179, 187 generation,

27, 48, 75, 76, 119, 190 glorify, 10, 11,

13, 26, 33, 114, 128, 204 glorifying, 61,

116

glory, 10, 11, 22, 24, 32, 33, 35, 37, 40, 42, 54, 59, 60, 61, 65, 85, 90, 99, 101, 103, 105, 114, 116, 121, 127, 129, 149, 169, 175, 190, 204, 206, 221, 222, 230, 231

God, 2, 3, 10, 11, 12, 13, 14, 15, 16, 17, 18, 20, 21, 22, 23, 24, 25, 26, 27, 28, 29, 30, 31, 32, 33, 35, 36, 37, 38, 40, 42, 43, 44, 45, 46, 48, 52, 53, 54, 56, 57, 58, 59, 60, 61, 62, 64, 65, 66, 67, 68, 70, 71, 73, 74, 75, 76, 77, 79, 80, 81, 84, 85, 86, 87, 88, 90, 91, 92, 93, 95, 96, 97, 98, 99, 100, 101, 102, 103, 104, 105, 107, 108, 110, 111, 112, 114, 116, 117, 118, 119, 120, 121, 122, 123, 124, 126, 127, 128, 129, 130, 131, 132, 133, 134, 136, 138, 139, 142, 145, 146, 147, 148, 149, 152, 154, 169, 170, 172, 173, 174, 175, 177, 178, 181, 183, 185, 187, 188, 190, 191, 192, 193, 197, 198, 199, 200, 201, 202, 204, 206, 209, 220, 221, 222, 225, 226, 228, 230, 231

Godhead, 32

gods, 10, 30, 113, 118, 121, 123, 199

good, 2, 10, 12, 16, 18, 24, 28, 38, 44, 45, 47, 48, 54, 61, 73, 76, 98, 102, 103, 104, 107, 109, 116, 138, 149, 158, 161, 163, 168, 169, 181, 182, 184, 191, 192, 199, 202, 221

goodness, 20, 86

gospel, 2, 61, 90, 173, 175, 181, 185, 207

governing, 42, 146

grace, 10, 32, 48, 61, 65, 80, 86, 87, 95, 97, 98, 99, 101, 175, 177, 181, 190, 195, 206, 209, 225, 229

grief, 75, 80, 82, 177, 179

hallowed, 127, 132, 201

heart, 10, 11, 15, 18, 23, 25, 33, 35, 53, 54, 57, 59, 82, 91, 92, 99, 110, 114, 116, 118, 147, 154, 155, 163, 169, 178, 179, 183, 197, 209, 225, 226, 231

heaven, 20, 21, 30, 36, 42, 57, 64, 66, 77, 78, 84, 103, 119, 121, 127, 130, 132, 133, 134, 143, 147, 166, 170, 178, 179, 180, 198, 200, 201, 202, 209, 226, 232

heinous, 170

hell, 56, 152

judgment, 48, 75, 76, 104, 105, 131, 152, 170, 177, 196

justice, 18, 20, 27, 29, 71, 75, 76, 107, 231

justification, 48, 93, 95, 101

kill, 150, 166

king, 70, 71, 78, 123, 200, 226

kingdom, 32, 54, 62, 71, 78, 79, 91, 101, 105, 127, 173, 187, 192, 201, 206, 207, 222, 226, 230, 231

knowledge, 22, 25, 40, 44, 48, 52, 75, 90, 101, 114, 169, 177, 196, 204

last day, 84, 91

law, 15, 44, 46, 48, 53, 58, 62, 65, 80, 82, 96, 99, 107, 108, 109, 131, 148, 169, 170, 172, 175, 176, 179, 183, 184, 198

lawful, 136, 138, 151, 157

life, 10, 11, 15, 17, 31, 44, 48, 50, 56, 57, 58, 59, 60, 61, 62, 64, 74, 76, 78, 80, 86, 92, 93, 99, 101, 104, 105, 106, 109, 128, 149, 151, 152, 163, 165, 169, 172, 173, 175, 177, 190, 199

Lord, 10, 12, 14, 21, 22, 24, 25, 26, 29, 30, 32, 36, 37, 40, 49, 59, 60, 61, 64, 70, 71, 73, 76, 79, 80, 84, 85, 88, 90, 92, 93, 95, 98, 99, 101, 103, 106, 110, 111, 112, 114, 124, 126, 128, 129, 130, 131, 132, 135, 145, 146, 147, 173, 176, 178, 181, 189, 190, 192, 193, 195, 196, 198, 199, 201, 202, 204, 206, 207, 220, 221, 225, 226, 227, 229, 230, 232

LORD, 10, 11, 14, 15, 17, 18, 20, 21, 22, 23, 24, 25, 27, 28, 29, 30, 35, 38, 40, 42, 43, 44, 45, 46, 48, 53, 56, 62, 64, 71, 75, 78, 79, 82, 84, 91, 107, 111, 114, 116, 118, 119, 121, 123, 124, 126, 127, 129, 130, 131, 132, 133, 134, 136, 137, 139, 142, 143, 145, 149, 158, 163, 165, 169, 177, 178, 179, 181, 183, 197, 198, 199, 202, 204, 209, 221, 222, 230, 231

Lord Jesus Christ, 32, 61, 64, 76, 80, 90, 93, 99, 101, 173, 206, 220

Scriptures, 13, 14, 15, 17, 83, 84

signs, 15, 74, 175, 187, 188

sin, 27, 46, 47, 48, 50, 52, 53, 55, 56, 59, 61, 62, 67, 68, 71, 75, 76, 90, 95, 98, 99, 100, 118, 169, 171, 172, 173, 177, 179, 183, 198, 225, 226, 228

sinful, 139

sinfulness, 52

sinned, 48, 50, 52, 54, 59, 166, 169, 177, 198, 230

sinner, 177, 178

sinners, 48, 52, 68, 96, 175, 181

sinning, 45, 46, 48, 206

sins, 42, 46, 50, 59, 67, 68, 76, 82, 83, 85, 90, 95, 100, 170, 173, 187, 190, 193, 197, 198, 225, 228, 230

slavery, 111, 203

Son, 15, 17, 31, 32, 57, 62, 64, 65, 67, 68, 70, 71, 74, 76, 78, 80, 81, 82, 85, 88, 105, 118, 134, 138, 166, 170, 175, 180, 187, 189, 190, 206, 226, 231

sons of God, 97

soul, 10, 11, 15, 18, 59, 67, 70, 75, 82, 91, 99, 110, 161, 199, 220

sovereignty, 123

special, 44, 201

Spirit, 14, 20, 21, 32, 33, 36, 53, 59, 61, 68, 70, 73, 74, 78, 79, 85, 86, 87, 90, 91, 92, 93, 98, 99, 101, 135, 173, 175, 180, 181, 187, 189, 190, 193, 202, 203, 206

spiritual, 14, 174, 183, 195

steal, 109, 156, 222

37979709R00137

Made in the USA
Columbia, SC
02 December 2018